PERSPECTIVES
ON EUROPE

PERSPECTIVES ON EUROPE

Proceedings of a Symposium
Held at Wellesley College
Under the Auspices of the
Barnette Miller Foundation

Edward A. Stettner, Editor

Arnulf Baring · Geoffrey Barraclough · Guido Calogero
Alexander Gerschenkron · Pierre Hassner · Jan Kavan
Charles P. Kindleberger · Ekkehart Krippendorff · Ugo La Malfa
Walter Laqueur · Kevin Mansell · Ivan Svitak · Willard Thorp
Lars F. Tobisson · Eric Van Loon · Otto Zausmer

SCHENKMAN PUBLISHING COMPANY, INC.
Cambridge, Massachusetts

CONTENTS

Contents

PREFACE

The following pages are the edited proceedings of a Symposium held by Wellesley College on April 1 and 2, 1969. The Symposium was the third in a series sponsored by the Barnette Miller Foundation, established by a bequest of Miss Barnette Miller, a former member of the History Department, "to provide for the advancement of the study [of] and research in International Relations. . . ." The Committee charged with directing the Foundation's affairs felt that Miss Miller's intentions might best be realized at present by assembling a group of distinguished experts, both American and European and with various areas of expertise, and asking them to take an intensive look at contemporary Europe.

Europe is today in a paradoxical situation. The dynamic economies of the various countries and their vital cultures seemingly guarantee that European influences are of world-wide importance. At the same time, in terms of military capacity and world-wide political power, Europe has obviously lost the preeminent position she so long enjoyed. In domestic politics, many Western European governments and political parties have recently been confronted with evidence of wide-spread popular dissatisfaction over very basic economic and social conditions. But none of these governments or parties has been able to do more than keep this dissatisfaction in check: no really successful reform movement of far-reaching effect has been generated anywhere. Eastern Europe continues to struggle toward greater autonomy, yet the still-developing Czechoslovak tragedy saddens the whole continent, perhaps putting an end to the search for détente of the last few years, and certainly leaving the foreign policies of East and West in flux. Even in the economic and cultural areas, questions and doubts arise. The future of the Common Market and the continuation of the economic prosperity of its members are at this date by no means free of obstacles. Also, Europeans are concerned that their economies and their culture may increasingly be coming to reflect American influences, and that economic independence and cultural identity may thus be slipping away.

The range and complexity of these questions regarding the condition of Europe required that our examination adopt several different perspectives, emphasizing several different factors. At the same time, the impossibility of isolating any of these factors from the others suggested the wisdom of a broad rather than a narrow focus. The chapters which follow present four broad perspectives on Europe.

Many of the specific questions raised in the later chapters are foreshadowed in chapter one, "What Does 'Europe' Mean Today?", which was intended as a prefatory overview. The general emphasis of the chapter is cultural, but the varying disciplines and backgrounds of the participants make for rather contrasting views.

Economic questions are the subject of the second chapter. The future of the European Economic Community (Common Market) is of prime interest here, but related issues such as the effect of recent disturbances on economic institutions, the status of Great Britain *vis a vis* the Market, and the place of Europe in the international economic system are considered.

The third chapter focuses on the social ferment of the last few years. Because students have played a leading role in this ferment, current and recent student leaders from various countries were asked to participate. The different national perspectives reveal different types of student organizations and conflicting analyses and evaluations of student involvement in society. Mr. Jan Kavan, a leader in the Czechoslovak student association, kindly agreed to contribute a postscript to this session, although he was for various reasons unable to accept our invitation to attend in person.

Chapter four examines the position of Europe in international politics. Special emphasis is given to the recent policy of détente undertaken by several Western European countries, and to the effect of the Czechoslovak invasion and subsequent events on this policy. Prof. Pierre Hassner also considers the broader question of how relations between European countries are affected by general East-West relations.

Events of the few months since the Symposium was held on April 1–2 have to some extent changed the nature of the questions then discussed. In particular, Charles de Gaulle, so dominant in early April, has been silent since his hasty resignation later that month. Still, de Gaulle's successors are obviously chary of so reversing his policies as to bring him forth from retirement. Indeed, none of the French policies examined in this book has yet been altered in any clear-cut fashion, and the questions of April have in no sense been answered. The September election in West Germany and the subsequent emergence of a new coalition may portend a change in German policy in some of the areas examined here, but again no clear indication of such a change has yet been given.

As this volume is the published record of a large Symposium, public recognition must be given to all who contributed to its success. Many members of the faculty, student body, and administration of Wellesley College were involved in planning the program and bringing it to fruition. Our thanks also go to Dr. Philipp Schmidt-Schlegel, German Consul-General in New York and a former member of Wellesley's faculty, and Prof. Dante Della Terza of Harvard University, for suggestions regarding the program, and to Mrs. Genevieve Childs and Mrs. Margaret Lee for their skillful typing of the manuscript. Kathryn Preyer, Associate Professor of History at Wellesley, is Co-Chairman of the Barnette Miller Foundation, sharing equally in the direction of this Sym-

Preface

posium and deserving much of the credit for its success. Lastly, the participants were most generous with their time and wisdom during the Symposium and in subsequently revising their remarks.

EDWARD A. STETTNER, Assistant Professor
of Political Science and Co-Chairman,
Barnette Miller Foundation

Wellesley, Massachusetts
October, 1969

INTRODUCTORY REMARKS

DR. RUTH M. ADAMS, President of Wellesley College: Good evening, ladies and gentlemen. On behalf of the College and the Barnette Miller Foundation, I take great pleasure indeed in welcoming to this Symposium the distinguished participants, the friends and the neighbors of Wellesley College who are here, and the members of the College—students, faculty and staff, trustees and the alumnae.

Miss Barnette Miller, who was Professor of History at Wellesley for 23 years, was a specialist on the Near East and was particularly interested in the Moslem world. Her interest in international relations led her to establish by a bequest to the College, a foundation to stimulate and assist at Wellesley the study of international relations both from a contemporary and an historical point of view. For this we are in continuing debt to her.

The Barnette Miller Foundation has had the pleasure of presenting two symposia in the past: one in 1960 on Africa and three years later one on Latin America. The Symposium on Africa was particularly important in that Africa was too little studied at that time. Many scholars argue that the same can be said of Europe in 1969. It's consequently our intention tonight and tomorrow to focus on the problems of contemporary Europe.

The program describes for you the plan of the Symposium and the notes tell something of the speakers, so in order not to repeat the printed material let us turn directly to the topic of the evening. The moderator will present to you the distinguished members of the panel. I, however, have the pleasure of presenting him, though

I believe he needs little introduction to this audience. Walter Laqueur is one of the foremost of contemporary historians. He has written more books and published in more journals than I can mention here. He is the director of the Wiener Library in London, and more happily for us is also our neighbor, teaching part of the year at Brandeis University. It is an honor and a great pleasure to present to you Walter Laqueur, Professor of the History of Ideas and Politics from Brandeis University, and our moderator for this evening's panel on "What Does 'Europe' Mean Today?" Professor Laqueur.

1

What Does "Europe" Mean Today?

PROF. LAQUEUR: This panel asks what does Europe mean today and what does it mean to be a European, which reminds me of Montesquieu's *Persian Letters,* where one character asks, "What does it mean to be a Persian?" Unfortunately, our assignment is a bit more difficult, because we are dealing not with a country but a continent.

Europe had been in a state of relative decline for a long time, and in 1945 it reached its zero hour. As a result of the destructions and the dislocations of the war, Europe was on the verge of economic disaster; it showed all signs of cultural exhaustion; and the countries of Eastern Europe had lost their political independence. Western Europe by that time was constituted of a number of small and medium sized countries which could not defend themselves and seemed no longer to be politically or economically viable.

The late Leon Trotsky once wrote that the European state system resembled the system of cages in an impoverished provincial zoo. Well, certainly in 1945 no one could quarrel with him. There were a great many prophets of doom at the time. For instance, Sartre wrote that Europe was dying in convulsions.

This is 1969, twenty-four years later. Twenty-four years is not a long time in history, but if you want to draw an interim balance, surely these twenty-four years have belied the predictions of most of the prophets of doom. There has been an astonishing economic

1

recovery, unprecedented in European history. Above all, this recovery has not been restricted to a small section of the population as so often before, but far larger sections of the various peoples and nations have benefitted.

Ten or fifteen years ago there was a lot of talk about the "third world," because all the new countries of Africa and Asia which had emerged no doubt constituted an important new force in world politics. But if you compare the situation today, the problems facing these countries of Africa and Asia, with the problems facing the countries of Europe, then no doubt European problems dwindle almost to insignificance. Again, ten or fifteen years ago many people talked about the prospect that these countries, perhaps in the near future, would outstrip Europe. I think now, in 1969, it seems that the real danger is that they will fall back even further. There is much to criticize as far as these achievements since 1945 are concerned. Prosperity has not only solved problems but it has also created new ones. There has been progress in Europe's economic cooperation, but very little in its political integration. But, everything considered, Europe has shown an astonishing amount of vigor and vitality. I think one could say that European ideas, European patterns, European techniques, are today spreading all over the globe, and that European civilization is imitated more or less successfully throughout the world.

In one sense, the European political predominance has ended. But in another sense, in a wider sense, the European age has only begun.

Prof. Laqueur then proceeded to introduce the panel, terming his own background cosmopolitan in that he was born in Germany, lived in France, and now divides his time between London and the United States. He remarked that his professional background, particularly writing a history of Europe since 1945, had convinced him of how little we really know of the continent. Professor Barraclough was introduced as a former President of the Historical

Association in London and a specialist in medieval and, recently, contemporary world history. Prof. Guido Calogero was introduced next, the chairman mentioning his role as co-founder of the Action Party, as well as his position at the University of Rome. Of Arnulf Baring, Prof. Laqueur noted that a list of his accomplishments in law, economics, history, philosophy, political science and radio work reminded one of Dr. Faustus in the famous prologue. It was also noted that Dr. Baring's new chair at the Free University was not likely to be a quiet position.

PROF. BARRACLOUGH: When you ask the question: "What does Europe mean today?" I think clearly your intention—or at least one intention—is to avoid those lengthy and learned but sometimes rather tiresome disquisitions about the history, or the historical background, of European unity, with which we are all probably a little too familiar. With this intention I am entirely in sympathy. Far too much that has been written about the history of European unity is propaganda of a more or less crude sort; it is the work of men who are believers in the ideal of a united Europe—and in this, of course, they are perfectly justified —but who at the same time are using history to reinforce their plea for unity by seeking out movements and tendencies and forces in the past which seem to make a united Europe a logical, or necessary, or even a predestined outcome of a long historical process. In my view—and I suspect it is your view too—such arguments are irrelevant in the context of contemporary problems. What we are concerned with here and now is not whether European unity is or is not something inherent in history—the culmination of historical developments—but whether it is required by the conditions of our time and by the overriding needs of the twentieth century. So I think we shall judge it, in short, on pragmatic grounds and not by historical arguments.

Nevertheless I also doubt whether you can discount the historical factor altogether. *Historiam furca expellas . . .* pitchfork history out of the front door, and it will be all too apt to fly back

3

in through the kitchen window. For one thing, the present concern with European unity, the movement for a united Europe, the initiatives which led first of all to the European Coal and Steel Community, the Treaty of Rome and to the European Common Market, these were all the product of a particular historical situation. They were a response to the shattering experience of Hitler's war, to the blows, as Mr. Laqueur has said, not only to the European economy (productivity in 1945 was down to half the level of the years 1935–39) but also to the self-confidence and morale of Europeans; they were a response to a chaos both material and spiritual. When Europe emerged again in 1945, crippled and disorganized, it was plain that it had been overtaken and dwarfed by the two great superpowers on its flanks; and it was in this reaction against the dwarfing of Europe that the movement for European unity was born. At the same time, a very natural revulsion against the excesses of nationalism favored the growth of a European spirit. Because national policies had led Europe to the brink of destruction, European unity was seen not as a distant ideal, but as an immediate present necessity.

But of course all this is now a quarter of a century ago, and the serious question is whether, in the very different conditions of 1969, the historical circumstances which underpinned the European idea between roughly 1944 and 1947 still prevail. Karl Deutsch, for example (certainly no enemy of European unity), pointed out eighteen months or two years ago that the integration of Western Europe had virtually come to a "standstill"; he said that it reached a "plateau" in 1957 and 1958, but since then it had failed to take off from that plateau. And, more recently, Anthony Sampson has described it as "stuck at the stage of an uneasy customs union which may not even survive as that." "The men who a few years ago talked as Europeans," he added, "now talk again as Germans, Frenchmen or Belgians." When we ask: "What does Europe mean today?" these are facts that we have to take into account. History (as I said) cannot be so blithely shouldered aside, and one basic historical fact is the fragility and short life

4

span of the European idea, and its dependence on the special circumstances which called it forth, and, on the other side, the strength and the durability and the deep-rooted attachment of people to their national loyalties.

What, then, does "Europe" mean today? It certainly does not mean—I think this is a statement of fact, whatever one may like to think—a conscious opposition or hostility to the reality of nationality and national differences. In that sense, General de Gaulle was right when he said that if there were to be a Europe, then it could only be a "Europe des patries." Frenchmen, Germans, Italians, Englishmen (England is a special case, but I won't complicate matters by going into that) think of themselves as Frenchmen, Germans, Italians and Englishmen first, and only in the second place as "Europeans"—if they think of themselves as Europeans at all. The idea of being a European is a secondary consideration, an accretion, something (as you may say) superimposed on a basic loyalty to their own native land, each of which (in de Gaulle's words) has "its own spirit, its own history, its own language, its own misfortunes, glories and ambitions." And this means, inevitably, that relatively speaking it is a weak idea.

Historically, you will find that the idea of Europe, the sense of European identity, comes alive—but only really comes alive—when there is a threat which is, or something which can be regarded as, a threat not to this country or that country, but to the whole of Europe. Usually, but not always, it is a threat from outside. "The whole future of Europe" was saved (one historian tells us) when Themistocles defeated the Persians in 480 B.C. But it could come from within—from Louis XIV or from Hitler, for example—threatening to subjugate the rest of Europe to one particular country. Still, it is the external threat which really creates the sense of European identity: in the Middle Ages Islam (it has often been said that the idea of Europe was born in the Crusades), in the sixteenth and seventeenth centuries the Turks, in the nineteenth century (read, for example, Marx's articles in the New York *Tribune* around 1850 and 1851) Russia (and this, of course, raises the hotly debated question whether Russia is a European or, as Marx insisted, an Asiatic power), and after 1945 Russia again, or the Soviet Union. And since 1945 there has been another development as well—namely, growing tendency among Europeans (or at any rate among some Europeans) to define Europe in contradistinction to America, and that really means in effect to the United States because they clearly do not feel the same about Latin America—to contrast European civilization and American civilization, which in fact they regard as a threat to the distinctive values of European civilization.

Actually this fear of America, this fear of the American impact on Europe, this fear of the growing "Americanization of the world," reaches further back. You can trace it at least to the emergence of American preponderance after the First World War. The Dutch historian Jan Huizinga, for example, expressed it very vividly back in 1924. Americans, he complained, do not fully realize the necessity for Europe of "preserving its divisions into many nations." He protested against the "equalizing and leveling" and "uniformity" he saw as characteristic of American life. Culturally, he said, these things were a "danger" to "real civilization," which could only be safeguarded by "diversity." What Huizinga was emphasizing was the contrast—as he saw it—between America, with its standardization and uniformity and conformity, and Europe, with its cultural diversity; and his object—his purpose—was to save the latter from the encroachments of the former.

It is obvious, I think, that this is a very negative conception of Europe. It is defined not in terms of itself, but by contrast, by antithesis: by contrast to Islam, by contrast to Russia, by contrast to America. In other words, it is only the threat from an alien world that forces people to take account seriously of the common elements (or the alleged common elements) among the European peoples. Otherwise what Europeans feel is their diversity, the difference between Poles and Germans, the difference between Frenchmen and Englishmen. And for this very reason the sense

6

of European identity is also volatile and ephemeral. It remains strong only as long as the threat (or alleged threat) to Europe remains strong, and disintegrates as soon as the immediate incentive becomes less urgent. That, I think, is obvious today. The threat from the Soviet Union which Western Europeans thought they perceived in Stalin's day, has become steadily weaker since around 1957 and 1958, and the sense of unity in face of a common danger which that threat engendered has also become correspondingly weaker at the same time.

Nevertheless I do think that Huizinga was right in stressing the cultural aspect, for the one thing history has left Europeans with is a certain community of culture. Politically Europe does not exist; politically, whether we like it or not, the reality today is not a united but a divided Europe. Militarily, Europe is certainly not self-sufficient, and in spite of de Gaulle's dream of Europe playing the role of a "third force," holding the balance between the U.S.S.R. and the U.S.A., it seems very doubtful whether Europe will ever again become militarily self-sufficient. Economically too, we are easily misled by the enormous blanket of propaganda put forth on behalf of the Common Market. The Common Market, in plain fact, rests on voluntary agreements between its members, who are concerned with furthering their own national interests, just as one businessman makes a deal with another businessman; its basis in any case is cooperation between sovereign states. Moreover, it is certainly an open question whether Europe as an economic unit really makes sense in today's highly articulated world with a global economy. In any case, as Jean-Jacques Servan-Schreiber has pointed out recently, the Common Market is far more European in appearance than it is in reality. According to Servan-Schreiber's estimates, United States capital already controls something like 15% of the manufacture of consumer goods in Europe; it controls 24% of the European automobile industry, 20% of the European light electrical industry (radio, television, recording systems etc.); and, most important of all, the new electronic sector on which modern industry

7

depends, is firmly in American hands (between 80% and 95% of the production of the essential electrical components is vested in firms which are either American or American-controlled). Why businessmen who profess European ideals and claim to fear being swamped by America find it so much easier to link up with American than with other European firms, is a question I cannot answer; but its implications for the economic unity of Europe are obvious and need no emphasis.

When we turn to the cultural aspects, on the other hand, the position is very different. No doubt, the cultural facts are intangible, imponderable, and difficult to define; but they are real. I think it was A. J. P. Taylor who once said that the one fact which precisely defines Europe is the use of the major and minor diatonic scale. And no one—in spite of Gauguin and *japonaiserie* and *chinoiserie* and other exotic influences on European painting—can fail to distinguish European from African or from Asian art. In this sense Europe exists. Of course, within the European tradition, we all know there are national schools: among painters, among musicians, among writers. But there is also a single tradition which extends right across Europe from England to Russia. English writers from Shakespeare to Shaw, just like Russian writers from Pushkin to Pasternak, are a part of the European heritage. They are European figures, just as musicians like Elgar or Britten, like Tschaikovsky or Shostakovich, are unmistakably European figures.

I will not belabor a point which I think is quite obvious. European literature without Dostoevsky would be unthinkable—as unthinkable as European literature without Proust. It may be an old-fashioned point of view (I suspect it is an old-fashioned point of view) but to me it seems that if Europe means anything today, it is a system of values and a way of life. It's true that the years since 1945 have seen a reaction against these values, which I think in many ways is justified. Justified because Europeans were too confident of the superiority of their civilization, too willing to turn a blind eye to its defects, too ready to assume that their values

8

were the ultimate values. And that of course they are not. Islam, Buddhism, Confucianism, and eastern Christianity as well, have their own standards, their own appreciation of the place of the individual in God's universe, which are just as estimable and just as valid as the standards of the West. It still remains true, however, that the distinctive feature of Europe, expressed in its arts and literature, is a system of values centering round the worth of the human personality and the importance of the human individual; and this approach to perennial human problems, which the particular spirit of Europe evolved—and which, perhaps, that particular spirit alone was able to evolve—will survive because, once expressed, it has become the possession of all mankind. It is Europe's essential contribution to the world, the product as much of the hill-towns and the cities of Tuscany as of the villages of Cotswold England, of the valley of the Loire as of the vineyards on the banks of the Danube. "What is Europe?" that skeptic Bismarck once contemptuously asked, when he was threatened with European displeasure at his aggressions. "Many proud nations" was the answer. I think it was a good answer, an answer which expressed one central aspect of the European question: unity in diversity, cultural (or, if you like, spiritual) unity in political diversity, the consciousness of common standards which Bismarck was ignoring, and by ignoring, was threatening.

But there remain two further points, or two further questions which I will very briefly discuss before I stop. The first is that we must not press this cultural unity too far. If culturally Europe forms a distinct entity, a distinct civilization different from Asia, or Africa, or America, that is one thing. But it would be false logic to try (so to say) to extrapolate it, make it a stepping-off point for other forms of unity. In many respects Islam is more of a cultural unity than Europe ever was; but pan-Islamism has not prospered. And the same is true of the pan-Arab or the pan-African movements. Latin America's twenty republics are superficially at any rate more alike than the national states of Europe; but pan-Americanism has not been a notable success. To share in a common culture has no necessary political or other implications. And this is as true of Europe as it is true of the Middle East or any other part of the world. Finally—and this is my second point—there is the question of the present state of European culture. Is it, in fact, still a reality, with all the distinctive features which characterized it in the past, or has it become little more than a nostalgic historical reminiscence? And if the latter is the case (and I think there are a lot of indications that it is the case), what then are the indications that a new common European culture is arising to take its place?

Everyone, I suppose, knows that Europe has experienced not only a remarkable revival since the war—a revival almost unthinkable in 1945—but also that it has simultaneously undergone a profound social transformation. I don't think you will expect or wish me to discuss that in detail. It is certainly, as much as anything in the so-called "under-developed" world, a revolution of rising expectations. The distinctive feature of Europe, as contrasted with the underdeveloped world of Asia and Africa, is that those expectations have largely been realized—not, naturally, to the extent that everybody wants (that would be quite impossible), but statistically to a very substantial degree. Naples, if you visit it, is no longer a city of grinding poverty, of dirt and beggars and shoeless children, as it was only twenty years ago. More generally, wages are high and unemployment is low, sometimes non-existent. Affluence has come to Europe, and with it a European version of John K. Galbraith's affluent society. That again is something I don't need to discuss. Its effect is that the distinctive regional or national differences—the "diversity" in which Huizinga took such pride as the distinctive feature of Europe—is being wiped out. Everywhere the distinctive feature is the automobile—the Volkswagen, the Fiat, the Morris Minor—or the bathroom which actually works, the refrigerator, the television set, and the array of television masts towering above every town and every village. And the really significant fact is the rise to pre-eminence, as the index of the new society, of social classes which set more store by

10

these things than they do by the old traditional values. The plain fact is that Huizinga was an old-fashioned comfortably well-off, middle-class liberal who had a nostalgia for the Europe of the past. The new classes have their sights set on very different things, and if this involves "Americanization" they do not mind—in fact, so much the better. That is why, I think, the attempt which has been made and is still made in Europe, to raise the American bogey, now that the Russian bogey has gone stale, this attempt of old-fashioned liberals and conservatives to play upon the alleged American threat to European civilization, is a non-starter. What people want, what most people want, what the now predominant social groups want (that is to say those groups politicians have to take into account when it comes to counting votes) is not less but more Americanization. They wish to catch up in all material things on the United States; they prefer American films to European films; they take their cultural as well as their material standards from America.

Now all this—and of course a great deal more which I must leave unsaid—has important bearings on what we mean by Europe today. It means at least the attrition of most things an older generation associated specifically with the word "Europe." I have no doubt of course that behind the superficially similar urban and suburban landscapes of Europe, there are still persistent underlying differences. That is beyond doubt. The question is: which are the most important, the similarities or the differences? And the impression I have is that the balance, which formerly favored the latter, favored the differences, is now tilting (if it has not already tilted) in favor of the former, the similarities. I am not even sure—but I am no expert in modern art in any of its forms— whether in the age of twelve-tone music and abstract painting, there is any longer any distinctive "European style." It may be— it has often been argued—that this new postwar trend towards uniformity, the emergence of a common style of living, will pave the way towards a united Europe by weakening or obliterating the old regional ties and loyalties. I do not know the answer any

11

more than any of you know the answer. Certainly, it does seem to me, there *is* a more "integrated" culture in Europe than there was at, let us say, the end of the nineteenth century. But whether that culture in any specific sense is a "European" culture is another question. Rather, it seems to me, it represents a European adjustment to a culture, to a way of living, that is rapidly becoming worldwide.

In this sense, it may truthfully be suggested that Europeans today are becoming less, not more European. That doesn't mean of course that they may not accept a measure of cooperation for economic reasons; but if they do, it will be a rational decision taken on commonsense, practical grounds, and will have nothing to do with the existence of a "European consciousness." Europe, as Paul Valéry long ago pointed out, is not a natural unit, geographically, politically or even economically. Europe is only a projection of Asia, a peninsula at the western end of the great land mass which we call the Old World. In an age when the stupendous development of communications is linking the whole world together, when distance is shrinking and the economies of all continents and hemispheres are more interdependent than ever before, when all the forces of science and technology are making for global integration, and when the world is already too small a place for its teeming populations, the idea of European integration sometimes looks more like an anachronism than a bold solution for the problems of the twentieth century. If it is anachronous, as advocates of the idea of European union often tell us, to think of ourselves any longer as Germans or British or French, it may also be no less anachronous to think of ourselves as Europeans. What we are in fact is citizens of the world; and we may be sure that what takes place in Asia and Africa, in China and India and Nigeria and the Middle East, will affect our lives as closely, in the integrated world of the twentieth century, as what takes place in Europe. We do not need to deny our distinctive "Europeanness"; there is no reason why we should; but it is not the most important thing in the world in which we live.

What Does "Europe" Mean Today?

PROF. CALOGERO: The question "What does Europe mean today?" should, in my opinion, be answered first of all by saying that Europe is a name which has many meanings. It may identify on the one hand just a geographical section of the world. On the other hand, it may suggest a will to reach a political unity on that continent. The problem is therefore not so much that of ascertaining the true meaning of the word as that of choosing the best one, of choosing the meaning which is most illuminating for the moral and political action which has to follow.

The idea that words have meanings which we have only correctly to determine is indeed one of the most naive assumptions of contemporary analytical philosophy. Such an assumption may be true for very simple names or very simple things, such as, for instance, cat or chair. It would not then be very sensible to answer the order, "Get that cat out of the chair," by some new questions, such as "What do you mean by chair, what do you mean by cat?" However, the more the meaning of the word which is investigated is rich and controversial, the more the questions in the form, "What does Europe mean?" have to be superseded by questions in the form, "What do you mean about Europe?" Consequently, when you speak with people with a sufficient knowledge of the language they are using, you will get many different answers, each of which will be justified from the point of view of the speaker. You will then have to choose among those various meanings and interpretations, not according to a sort of platonic eternal dictionary of ideas and meanings, but according to what you think to be the best interpretation to be given and the best action to be followed.

I therefore think that my friend Altiero Spinelli, who is one of the most experienced Europeans as far as problems of European federation is concerned, is quite right when he quotes, in the very beginning of the preface to his book *Rapporto sull'Europa* (Milan, 1965), the answer given by the French statesman Jean Monnet in 1952. Monnet, who was expecting to take over the authority of the just-born European Coal and Steel Community, answered

13

squarely: "Europe is that bit of united Europe which we have been able to build now. It will be tomorrow that which we will be able to build tomorrow."

I would therefore start from this point. Europe is first of all what we want it to be. In other words, it is a mistake in my opinion to emphasize first the problem of the cultural, historical, spiritual or even the racial unity of Europe, as if to assume that a human community might become a state only if it had such a pre-existing unity. If this principle were true, we in Italy would never have achieved political unity, because a cultural unity simply did not exist in Italy before its political unification approximately a century ago.

Of course we had had, for many centuries before that unification, great Italian literature, written from the times of Dante and Petrarch and Boccaccio in a slightly refined form of the usual dialect spoken in Tuscany, and especially in Florence. But the fact that from those times, that is from the 14th until the beginning of the 19th century, Italian writers and poets went on using more or less the same literary language adopted by Dante and Petrarch and Machiavelli, was a question meaningful to only a few thousands or at the most a few tens of thousands of people all over Italy. The great majority of the Italians of even the 19th century were illiterate, and so unable to read and to understand those poets and writers and therefore to possess a common culture. Also, very few inhabitants of any of the small states or foreign colonies into which Italy was divided could have understood the dialect spoken by the inhabitants of most of the other small states. The political unity of Italy, which has never been challenged since unification in 1861 (1870 for Rome) was indeed the result of very strong and independent actions of a few strongly committed men, such as Mazzini, Cattaneo, Garibaldi, and Cavour, who at the very end was able to bring the process to a happy conclusion with the help of Napoleon III, Emperor of France, and Victor Emmanuel II, King of Piedmont.

Of course, action by those men and maybe a dozen others was

supported by what we may call liberal opinion in Italy. But this too represented only some hundreds of thousands of cultivated Italians, and certainly not the great majority of the illiterate population of Italy at the time. So when Italy was unified in 1861, Massimo d'Azeglio, Piedmontese politician and writer, said that Italy had been made but Italians were still to be made.

Certainly Americans at the time of the *Federalist* were not as illiterate as their contemporaries in Italy. But the creation of the United States was also the result of the cooperation of a few great men. We do not need to go to Philadelphia and read the original text of the Constitution of the United States of America in order to know what these men have done for the greatness of your country and for the future of the world.

For Europe, in my opinion, it will be the same. Europe will be unified only if the political leaders of its nations decide to go that way. They do not, in my opinion, have to discuss in advance whether there is or is not a cultural unity in Europe. After all, such a unity does exist in Europe in many senses in which it does not exist within some European nations. A Milanese is more similar to an inhabitant of Munich than to a peasant of some parts of Southern Italy, just as a citizen of Marseilles is more similar to a citizen of Genoa than to a citizen of Paris, despite any dream of national *grandeur de la France*.

There is also, I think, an important opposing example. The only real example of great cultural unity in Europe—and this is exactly an example for which we cannot think of any political unity following that cultural unity—is the cultural unity of all German-speaking people in Europe. All the people in the three Germanys, the Federal one, the Popular Democratic one, and Berlin, and also the people in Austria and the German-speaking people of Switzerland, speak the same language with only slight differences in dialect. And as far as written German is concerned, there is really one language. But we could never think of such a thing as the unification of German-speaking people in Europe, for this would be to commit Hitler's mistake, which would now be

15

quite impossible from the point of view of the political picture of the whole world.

So you have cases in which you have cultural unity and no political unity build upon this cultural unity, or you may have strong political unities (for instance, the Italian) which have not been built on a previous cultural unity. In this sense, I would say the responsibility for the making of Europe belongs not only to the leaders of the European nations, but also to the Americans. It would have been useless to save Europe from a hegemony or a dictatorship twice in a century with the lives of so many American boys, and then refrain from strong action towards European unity only because some old man, dreaming of the glory of his country, still suffers from the sickness of chauvinism.

PROF. BARING: I will limit myself to some small remarks about my feeling about being a European, especially being a European Socialist, and more specifically being a German Social Democrat from the smallest of the three states which Prof. Calogero mentioned, that is, Berlin. I don't belong to the New Left, and I wouldn't say I quite belong to the Old Left. I'm sort of in between these two states, which perhaps is a question of age, and I think I should speak to you about the feeling of frustration one has today being European.

Of course, everybody in this world is frustrated, and the experience of failure is, I think, part of human life. In a more historic or political sense, America lives today through a period of frustration, and the Vietnam War which has opened new and perhaps tragic dimensions to American political life may enable you to understand what I'm talking about. Comparing the American example today with the European experience of the last two decades, I think it is possible that you experience for the first time the limitations and failures of politics and the complete political stalemate which I see in Europe today.

Regarding Europe, I may begin by repeating and enlarging

upon the geographical question. It is quite easy to distinguish Australia from Asia, or to differentiate North America from South or Latin America, which starts south of the Rio Grande, but in the case of Europe it is really very difficult. How about the islands like England or Ireland or Iceland? How about Americans? General de Gaulle, as you know, has said that America is the daughter of Europe, which saying, of course, is very much attuned to his mind, but perhaps not so much to American feelings, or to the realities of today. We feel (in my generation at least) much more like children of the United States. But if you analyze for a moment the feelings towards Europe which Americans have had in their history, and which they still have or which they may have again, I would underline the common culture which exists. Walking over the Wellesley ground, or living in Boston, or going to Harvard, or New York (California may be different), you feel and you see and you sense in every theater, movie and concert, that this is part of Europe. Or that we are—all of us—part of this Atlantic community which stretches from some place in Europe, perhaps the Ural hills (which de Gaulle cherishes so much and which are not higher than Mt. Washington in the White Mountains, and so not really a dividing line) to some place perhaps in the middle West or even in California. But what does it mean in terms of politics?

You all know that since the time of Washington's Farewell Address there has been a specific and very deeply-rooted aversion in America towards Europe, sometimes a contempt, often a distaste for Europe and European politics. When Wilson in the First World War, or Franklin Roosevelt in the Second, tried to and were successful in liberating Europe, they tried to put it in its place again and then to leave. They didn't want to be involved, and when America was involved after the Second World War, it seemed really to be a breaking—a turning point in American history. I say it seemed to be, because I feel that today this strong feeling of being responsible for Europe, this mixture of pity and

17

impatience you had for Europe, is going to disappear, and that perhaps something like impatience and a bit of boredom, as Stanley Hoffman has put it, may prevail.

Another question to consider is: "Does Russia belong to Europe?" I think we should discuss this because England is represented here by Mr. Barraclough, but nobody from Eastern Europe or from Russia is taking part in our discussion. As someone from Berlin, I feel much closer to Eastern Europe and to Russia, geographically at least, than some of the others here could. Does Russia really belong to Europe? It is not an academic question because if, as Mr. Barraclough has pointed out, the Soviet threat is becoming weaker and weaker we must realize we speak only of Western Europe; it is not so for Eastern Europe. And Poland, Czechoslovakia, Hungary, Rumania and Bulgaria belong as much to Europe as all of us in the western or the central part of Europe. This eastern part of Europe, as events of last year have demonstrated, is still under Soviet domination, and certainly is going to be under Soviet domination for some time. So the answer to this question, does Russia belong to Europe, depends on the way you look at it. From Berlin, Prague or Warsaw, it looks rather Asiatic, from China it looks certainly very European. In practical terms, of course, it doesn't matter, as Mr. Barraclough has pointed out, if the threat is coming from within or without; it is a threat for the center of Europe and a daily reality for the eastern part of Europe to live with dominating Russian power. As far back as we can go in history, Europe, a loose community of nations, has always resented being dominated by one power; and it isn't any better being dominated by two powers. But of course there are remarkable differences between being dominated by the United States and by the Soviet Union, otherwise I wouldn't be here.

If you understand that for the first time Europe is not capable of freeing herself from this Soviet domination, you will appreciate the remarkable differences compared with the time of the Turks, the attempts of Napoleon the First to make France the leading power in Europe, or Hitler's experience which we all lived through

18

30 years ago. For the first time Europe is not capable of being herself, and the attempts Gen. de Gaulle has made have underlined, I think, the failure of European attempts to free herself and to be herself once again.

So there you have the basic feeling of frustration. Outlining it a bit more as far as Eastern Europe and Central Europe are concerned, you all know and have noticed tremendous changes which have been going on in Eastern Europe in the last decade, beginning after Stalin's death. We have all lived through this experience of suddenly noticing new life under the cover Stalin imposed in 1945, the reemergence of national independence, of revisionism, of liberalization in some if not all parts of Eastern Europe. And having introduced myself here as a European Socialist or Social Democrat, I think I should say a few words about the feelings we had (Americans of course have had the same feelings, but perhaps to a lesser degree) looking at Europe in the last year.

I think the developments which took place last spring, just a year ago, in Czechoslovakia have had a tremendous impact on all of us. For Socialists (and that of course doesn't mean being communists, but rather people trying to find a combination of freedom and socialism in this century), the tremendous impact of the Czech attempt and then of the Czech failure has been the fact that this was a chance to overcome, within the limits of Soviet and American domination, the division between the eastern and western parts of Europe. Some of us felt skeptical but hopeful that it could be possible to find a combination of a more liberal East, emphasizing the Bill of Rights and particularly the rights of the first amendment of the American Constitution plus some kind of constitutional review, and the West. The West is now becoming, in all countries including the United States, more socialist, that is, it is expanding social justice, health services, old age pensions and all kinds of programs to make this world not only safe for democracy but for justice, liberty and equal opportunity for all of us. When this attempt failed last August, tremendous hopes were destroyed, or at least delayed for a long time to

19

come. The feeling of frustration in Czechoslovakia, of hatred of the Soviet Union, and, I think, of some disappointment in the United States, is a characteristic of today's political climate in the center of Europe, and not in Czechoslovakia alone. I don't mean that anybody expected the United States to use atomic power to prevent the Russians from invading Czechoslovakia. We all know that the first part of the world which would be completely destroyed in such a case would be Central Europe. But we felt that some diplomatic means could have been used, and would have been used if America at the time had been closer to Europe, and if the pressures put on President Johnson by the Vietnam War and by his desire to go to Moscow before the end of his term were not as strong as they apparently were. And so, any American going to Prague this summer should be prepared for discussion not only of Soviet intervention but also of American passivity. Which I think is part of the larger change in attitudes, which I described before as impatience on the one side and boredom on the other.

A few more words about this kind of frustration as found in my own country, in Germany. Of course the case is different. Czechoslovakia is perhaps the model state for the kind of experience I just described, but it's an extreme case. That is, the limitations on political possibilities are much more important in the Czech case than the German. But I think the common point (and perhaps this is true of France and Britain as well) is the inability of these countries to shape their own national destiny, to exercise their self-determination, which means that they are to a much lesser degree able to pursue their own policies and thus to create this new European Europe, which whether we are for de Gaulle or against de Gaulle we all hope to see one day.

PROF. LAQUEUR: Perhaps a short postscript is appropriate, since a number of points have been suggested by my colleagues. Czechoslovakia, for instance, is a good example of the emergence of a European conscience or consciousness. What happened there was far more acutely felt in Europe, in Western Europe, than in any other part of the world. It was really a great shock, even for people on the Left and the far Left. I remember talking to French or British Communists who were violent in their denunciation of the Soviet Union. But Americans who were anything but Communists told me, "Look, don't get excited, after all, everyone knows this belongs to the Soviet's sphere of influence. And how important is Czechosolvakia anyway?" I wouldn't generalize too much from my own personal experience, but the point I want to make is that in an hour of danger this European consciousness emerges fairly clearly.

Now as far as the Soviet Union is concerned, I'm not absolutely sure, not as sure as Mr. Barraclough, that the danger is over. On the other hand, I'm more confident than Mr. Baring that the Soviet Union is part of Europe. I do not want now to enlarge General de Gaulle's conception—to say Europe to the Ussuri rather than the Urals—but there's no greater insult in talking to a Russian, especially to a Russian intellectual these days, than telling him he doesn't belong to Europe, because he's very proud of being an essential part of the European tradition.

How important is the cultural dimension? Is there such a thing as European culture? Have the national cultures become more similar? Well, if one compares the present with the Middle Ages, we have a very separatist and centrifugal culture. In the Middle Ages (Mr. Barraclough knows more about this than I), there was really one Europe because people had a common language, a *lingua franca*. There were not as many universities, and people were moving from London to Prague and from Prague to Salamanca. If they were not moving, they at least knew what was happening in the other place. And there were not so many books and periodicals published, so an educated man knew everyone else in his field—and not only in his field but in every field.

I grew up and graduated from school in the 1930's. I see a tremendous difference between this Europe of the 1930's and the Europe of the 60's. Wherever one goes in Europe, especially if one doesn't move too far from a railway station or from airports, there's a very similar scene. The cities are becoming more and more alike. The newspaper stands are becoming more and more alike. All over Europe, young people aged 18–20 as a rule now know foreign languages, and even go for a few months or even a year or two to live in another country. This was the exception not the rule before the Second World War. We have also this new phenomenon which was mentioned before, mass tourism. There are 24 million foreign tourists arriving in Italy each year and 18 million in Spain, and so on and so forth. This is something new —it never existed before. Traveling was a privilege of the rich. I'm talking not about high culture but mass culture, so to speak. There's a tremendous amount of cross fertilization, or whatever we call it. Sometime ago I was in Poland, and to my great surprise, I watched television, and what did I see—I saw "Dr. Finlay's Casebook." This will not mean anything to you, so let me say very briefly in explanation that it is a British, or to be precise the Scottish, Dr. Kildare, meaning a ruggedly handsome young man in a Scottish village who is a country doctor and has exploits running to about a hundred episodes. I can't think of anything more full of local color and full of references which would never be fully understood outside of Scotland, let alone outside Britain. But here it was on Polish television week after week, and the Poles were apparently enjoying it hugely.

Let's move for a moment to the higher ranges of culture. Here again, after the Second World War, wherever we look we can detect new trends, a tremendous amount of cultural traffic, so to speak. Brecht has been discovered in Britain and France, and so has Kafka. German philosophy has moved to the West. We have now musical congresses from Edinburgh to Salzburg; composers have become very very international. Everyone resides now in Baden Baden, including the Italians, including the French, and they move freely from one country to another. I needn't even mention science. True, at one time the Nazis tried to establish a German mathematics and German physics, and Stalin also played with this idea for a little time, but no one took it seriously. Scientists are really now members of a world republic.

The same goes for painting and sculpture. If we look for a moment to see who are or were the main members, who are the most representative members of what is now called *Ecole de Paris*, we have Lanskoi and De Stael who are Russians, and we have Vasareli who is a Hungarian, and Hartung who is a German, and Michaux who is a Belgian and so on. Admittedly one shouldn't press this point too hard, because in some respects, I think especially in literature, in *belles lettres*, there has been no such trend. Perhaps it could even be argued that European literatures have become more different than they used to be. National character is perhaps more important today than it was.

I'm not absolutely sure what follows from all this in political terms. It may well be that in the short range it is not really very important, because whether people draw closer or not culturally does not necessarily have immediate political repercussions. I'm not so sure about the more distant future. And it may well be that politically and culturally and economically Europe is moving much closer. I remember having seen border markers, I think it was between Belgium and Holland or between Holland and Germany, which were signs reading "Another Border but still Europe." So, probably, in a long-term view, these cultural trends are of some significance.

Professor Calogero was asked how he reacted to Professor Barraclough's paper.

PROF. CALOGERO: I agree with Professor Barraclough inasmuch as he says that we are not all citizens of the world, that this is not a political reality, and it won't be for a long time ahead. Another very serious point which Professor Barraclough made is that Europe is now in a way obsolete. The real problem is Atlantic community. Thus, he argues we have no longer to anticipate the political unity of Europe but rather a political unity of Europe plus the United States of America. Is this really, though, a contemporary political problem? I doubt it.

Prof. Barraclough was asked if China would eventually provide an external threat of such magnitude as to unite Europe.

PROF. BARRACLOUGH: I certainly don't regard China as a threat to Europe. Much as distance has contracted, it doesn't seem to me to have contracted to that degree. What China may be in 50 or 60 years, I don't know, no one knows, but in the foreseeable future I cannot see that China in any direct sense is a threat to Europe. In fact, I deprecate the whole revival of the Yellow Peril scare which once was popular, and which seems to me to exaggerate things which I think aren't worth exaggerating. If China is a threat to anyone, it is to Russia. It's a threat to little bits of European possessions like Hong Kong, but everyone knows that Hong Kong will revert to China. But in the case of Russia, there are substantial areas of territory at play and this may be a threat not to Russia as a European power but to Russia as a continental power stretching across from Europe into Asia. Of course, any threat to Russia on its Asian side is in one sense a threat to Europe, but only indirectly.

Professor Baring was asked to comment on the student demands at Berlin's Free University.

PROF. BARING: Basically, what is happening in Berlin today is similar to what is happening in all universities of the West. We would have to inquire what the students want if we are to answer this question. I would like to emphasize one point which I think was made very well in last Sunday's *New York Times Magazine* by Stephen Spender, namely that there is a difference between what the Czech students wanted last year and still want and what our students want. I am very much for university reform and

24

have taken active part in it, but I'm more and more disappointed about the students' vagueness. I feel that the desire to create anarchy is more and more obvious these days, and that students' perspectives and their desires to reform and really to achieve something in this field (and a university is a political institution in this sense) are weaker and weaker, not only in my country but in yours and in France.

On the one hand, I feel that the Czech students have been with and among the best and the most progressive part of the population. On the other hand, I feel that the students in our countries try to isolate themselves from everybody else and try to have as many enemies as possible. Liberal professors in particular, who should be closest to them, are considered their worst enemies. It was different in Czechoslovakia. And it was intelligent to be different in Czechoslovakia, because liberal professors, modern artists, writers and students were trying to make and to have the same thing, a more modern and more open, more just society.

Thus, I'm very much for the Czech students, and while I'm open to the students of our countries, I'm more critical of them.

Prof. Baring was then asked if he distinguishes between a Central European and a Western European consciousness.

PROF. BARING: I certainly feel that it is different living in Prague or Berlin, from living in London or Paris or Rome. I think it is quite characteristic of the situation, that from Professor Barra-clough's point of view the Soviet threat has really diminished. From my point of view it has not. Two years ago the University of Berlin had a seminar jointly with French students from Paris. Mr. Raymond Aron and his students came to Berlin and our students met with them, talking about the end of the cold war. It was very interesting that the French underlined the possibilities of a new era after the cold war; the Germans were much more skeptical. I don't think this has anything to do with German stubbornness, but it's just the situation. If you are in the center of

Europe, and if half of your country, justly or unjustly, is under Soviet domination, and if Berlin is encircled by Russian troops, you feel quite differently about it than if you live in Paris, where de Gaulle tries to reestablish diplomatic and even friendly relations not only with Eastern Europe but with the Soviet Union as well. I can go further and say that partly because of this differing perspective, a common framework of Western policy towards the Soviet Union is more and more lacking. We have no connection whatsoever between American foreign policy in relation to the Soviet Union and the French and the British and to some extent German policy. This is really a difference which stems largely from the geographical condition.

Prof. Laqueur was asked for his views on European integration.

PROF. LAQUEUR: Well, my colleagues will surely give their own answers, but my feeling is that European unity (the degree of unity would have to be discussed) for any number of political and economic reasons is not only desirable but essential. Take simply the economic considerations which will be emphasized later in this Symposium. The economies of small countries are simply not viable unless there is the closest collaboration. They are unable to undertake major projects, the whole business of research and development. In addition, of course, issues of defense come in, and here I think a very strong case can be made for more European unity. This does not, however, necessarily mean a United States of Europe on the American pattern.

PROF. BARRACLOUGH: I would like to comment on this question about the value of a united Common Market, and whether European unity is desirable, because I take a slightly different view from Mr. Laqueur. Naturally, it's very difficult as a general proposition to deny that European unity is desirable, but it does of course depend very much on what you mean by European unity. It's very clear that close union between certain parts of

What Does "Europe" Mean Today?

Europe can mean a greater disunity between those parts of Europe and other parts. One of the great dangers I think of the partial unity of Europe, as now represented by the countries of the Common Market, is that those countries may line up against the other countries or vice versa. In fact, what you may get both economically and otherwise is a sort of contest between the two halves rather than real unity. If by the unity of Europe you are talking about the unity of every part of Europe, including Spain, for example, right through to the Ural Mountains, that is one thing. If you're talking about partial unities, which imply differences between different parts of Europe, this unity could—I don't say would—but it could accentuate differences rather than produce a real unity.

That really leads me to another point. I said that Europe is not self-sufficient in military affairs. Then we need to ask, do Europeans themselves realize this and acknowledge a need for American military defense? If so, how do they justify the American presence? The answer to this, of course, is that it is misleading to talk of Europeans—do Europeans do this, do Europeans do that. Europeans are just as divided among themselves as Americans are. Some Europeans, particularly the followers of General de Gaulle, take the view that Europe can and should be militarily self-sufficient. My own view is that Europe can't and won't, but that's only my view against General de Gaulle's. But there are very good reasons why I hold my view—the gap for example in atomic weapons is immense. It could hardly ever be closed whatever Europe could do, even if it were to unite. So most Europeans do acknowledge a need for American defense, but that does not mean that there are not important political divisions. For example, in the Federal Republic of Germany there is much greater recognition of a belief in the need for American defense than there is in France. I believe in England the position probably is much more evenly balanced, with the government, whichever party it is, always coming out on the side of having American troops in England, and the population very often having different views.

27

Regarding the justification of the American presence—well, if you've got an American presence you accept it, just as presumably the East Europeans accept a Russian presence. But I do think, as Professor Baring emphasized, that Europeans do feel both the American presence and the Russian presence. They feel, as he rightly said, limited in their own control over their political destinies, and this *can* be a frustrating thing. The surprising thing to me is the degree to which it isn't. That I think is due to the very satisfactory economic situation—the great improvement in the economic situation. If that ever were reversed, I believe you could have a very swift reversal of the feeling about American influence, and as Prof. Baring says a much greater sense of frustration.

The question whether student revolts either promoted or delayed European unity was then raised.

PROF. LAQUEUR: I don't think they have a great effect, but in a way, which Hegel would have called the cunning of reason, European unity is helped along by the efforts of Messieurs Cohn-Bendit and Dutschke insofar as this new movement has its international connections. The students apparently experience a great deal of international solidarity, and who knows, in a roundabout and indirect way this too may contribute to European unity.

Prof. Calogero was asked whether American meddling would not hinder rather than aid the development of a European consciousness, and whether several strong leaders could achieve this unification.

PROF. CALOGERO: I do not want a separate, unique identity for Europe. What I would like to see in Europe is the different nations (keeping their diversities) uniting in one nation, just as the United States united. Americans helped Europe twice in a very important way in this century, and I think they should not

28

be shy about doing all they can in order to bring Europe towards unity.

Regarding the role of political leaders, I believe that Europe would proceed slowly but surely. towards unity if only one European leader would not be opposed.

One thing more. When I was the director of the Italian Institute in London, from 1950–1955, it seemed that all over Europe there was a desire to have unity; the only nation which did not agree was Great Britain. I remember that I told many friends in Britain that the time would come when they would want a united Europe, but by then they would be asking for admission, instead of being asked. Now in my opinion, the real willingness of the European nations to have unity would be proven by the acceptance of Great Britain. This is the real test. Another real test would be to have each European nation make absolutely compulsory the study of English together with the national language. All Europeans should learn to speak English, and this would be the best way to show that the Italians, the French, and the rest are not nationalistically inclined. Of course we should perhaps ask the English, in order to be just, to learn another language.

PROF. BARING: I would like to disagree with Professor Calogero on a few points. I agree with his intentions that a united Europe would be something nice and good. I disagree I think with all points he made as far as analysis is concerned. The facts are just different. Americans shouldn't be shy in pushing European states towards union, and they haven't been shy since the Second World War. But the outcome is a rather pessimistic picture. You can do what you want, and the Europeans will stay what they are— Europeans, that is, not united. There is no union of Europe now and there won't be a union of Europe in the foreseeable future. This is quite clear and it has nothing to do as far as I can see with General de Gaulle. If you removed de Gaulle from the European scene, it wouldn't make a difference. France and fifty million Frenchmen think much more like de Gaulle does than I would like to admit, because I agree with your intentions, as I said. France is much more Gaullist than Italians and Germans and the Netherlands and Belgium often think. And without France, of course, there can't be any union in Western Europe. So there won't be any.

Also, if you look at Italy or Germany, as soon as a basic concern is touched, as soon as an essential question is discussed in the Common Market, for example agricultural affairs, these countries tend to defend their national interest or what they believe to be their national interest on very narrow terms. They are not at all prepared to give up any of the rights they have kept until now. Even if their rights in general terms have diminished, and sovereignty doesn't mean as much any more as it did perhaps 50 years ago, they defend what they have.

I think the only chance Europe has for unity is to unite against one threat. Yet I'm quite happy that Europeans feel that the threat facing them in Western Europe is so much smaller than it was 15 or 20 years ago that they don't have to unite. Indeed, as far back as the early 1950's some Europeans—and I think these were more intelligent in analyzing the situation than others—felt European union wasn't necessary because Soviet Russia wouldn't attack them militarily. If there is no threat of attack they won't unite. If, for example, the United States should have domestic problems of a tremendous order, and if American guarantees for Europe should then not mean anything, and if at the same time the Soviet Union should try to exploit this situation, then Europe would no longer quarrel about the costs of military expenditures. Americans have, of course, always resented the fact that we want to be protected but not to pay; in this hypothetical case, we suddenly would pay. But this would mean a tremendous change inside Europe only because of the immediate threat. And another result would be extreme imbalance in the domestic structures of our countries. This would mean, I think, a turn to the political Right, the very conservative military-minded. So I'm quite happy that we don't have this need for union.

What Does "Europe" Mean Today?

PROF. CALOGERO: I shall answer that I am not particularly versed in economic questions. But as far as I know, in Italy the Common Market is going on rather well, in spite of some difficulties in the agricultural field. But agriculture has never determined the life of a country. It's far more important that automobiles are now built in Italy and sold in Germany or built in Germany and sold in Italy. The same is true of other products. But every time the Europe of the Six convened in order to take another step, France was the only opposition. The responsibility for the lack of unity in Europe is France's. I think the United States of America should do this as far as France is concerned: it should not be too shy towards France. I am really astonished to see such a great nation as the United States of America, with great achievements in every field of human activity, including fiction and poetry and arts, and of course science and technology—I am astonished to see this nation still regarding Paris as the center of the world. This is rather ridiculous, and it is exploited by the political forces which still dream of Paris as the center of Europe. I have nothing against France. Indeed, in Italy, in 1940, when Mussolini acted as he did against France, our faces were red with shame. In that moment to listen to General de Gaulle on the radio was for all of us in Italy a great moment. So I pay tribute to General de Gaulle as a man of the resistance, as the man who saved the honor of France. But at the same time, I must say that now he is just fighting against what has to come, that is, the unity of Europe.

PROF. BARRACLOUGH: I don't want to be left out of this debate about General de Gaulle. Like Professor Baring, I find myself really very very much in opposition and contradiction to Professor Calogero. I'm sorry he has placed so much emphasis on General de Gaulle, because in this country it is already almost an *idée fixe* that General de Gaulle is the only obstacle practically to everything. If you believe that, then you're going to be in for a terrible deception. General de Gaulle in many respects stands for France; in a remarkable degree General de Gaulle stands, as

31

Professor Baring says, for 50 million Frenchmen. That's not far from the truth. Therefore the notion that General de Gaulle alone stands in the way of a European unity which otherwise would come about almost overnight is not a realistic view of the situation.

I quoted Karl Deutsch before as saying that there has been no progress beyond the level of 1957–1958 as far as the purely economic aspects of European unity go. The question is much more whether one believes that this progress is desirable. Here I would commend to you the thoughts of Professor Baring, because I believe this is a far more open question than most people are apt to think. The benefits and the disadvantages can be seen from several points of view. Why the United States should feel any compulsion to press Europe to unite is not clear. When it did so in the past the reason was obvious, but it is no longer. In fact, this pressing for unity seems to me a very unlikely thing for United States to do politically, seeking, as it is, a détente with Russia.

Another point. Economically, one of the reasons for selling Volkswagens in Italy and Fiats in Germany is to make quite sure that you don't sell Fords and Chryslers in either country. The United States has a wonderful way of avoiding this problem by buying itself into the European motor market. But from the United States' economic point of view, united Europe is a very dubious proposition, unless United States capital is somehow involved. This is well known as one of the great ambivalences in President Kennedy's attitude towards a united Europe.

PROF. LAQUEUR: I'm not absolutely convinced I agree. I think I side with Professor Calogero. De Gaulle's policy has been a disaster, from the French point of view, too. Of course, there is strong French resistance against Europe, there is resistance in every country. But after de Gaulle there will be a chance at least to discuss it again. The conflicts which exist can perhaps be settled, as the conflict about agricultural production was settled. One should say in fairness that de Gaulle has not always been the main obstacle; in the first 7 or 8 years it was Britain who was the main culprit, and if Churchill had the brilliant idea first he was also the first to get cold feet.

Economic interests were in the beginning very distrustful of the Common Market, but I think they soon realized the benefits which would accrue to them. With some notable exceptions, especially agriculture which has to be protected, economic circles have recently been much more enthusiastic than political circles.

Prof. Laqueur was asked to discuss the effect of the Czecho-slovak invasion on the Western European attitude towards the Soviet Union.

PROF. LAQUEUR: Czechoslovakia has brought about changes in this attitude. Some people think that Czechoslovakia was an unfortunate episode. The French Foreign Minister, for example, said it's very unfortunate, but if an accident has happened in a certain street, it doesn't mean that we have to close the road. I'm afraid, however, that this parallel is not quite exact. Rather, it seems to me the ground under the street has subsided a little bit, and it would be dangerous in the future for any cars to pass through. What I mean is this: for the last four or five years Western Europeans have been very optimistic. There was hope that the détente would go on, that there would perhaps be a European security pact of sorts, that Russia would gradually become more Europeanized, that the Russian hold on the East European countries would erode slowly, and that Western and Eastern Europe could slowly establish ties.

Russian action in Czechoslovakia has unfortunately shown that this was a kind of false symmetry between West and East, that while the United States did not impose its will on dissenting allies in Europe (perhaps because it didn't want to, perhaps because it couldn't do so), the Soviet Union had both the resolution and the ability to keep its clients or allies or whatever they call them together. Another result has of course been the Brezhnev doctrine, which says that all East European countries are sovereign, but that there's an overriding interest of socialism or communism, which only the Soviet Union can interpret, and which gives it the right to intervene whenever necessary.

It may well be that this doctrine should be taken with a pinch of salt, but it acts as a deterrent in Western Europe, and has postponed any real progress towards a new détente. There is still a common interest in preventing a new war, but this alone is not enough. Real coexistence such as appeared possible after Cuba— this I fear has receded to the distant horizon.

The European Economy: Prospects for Unity?

PROF. GERSCHENKRON: Let me first make a few general remarks before turning to the panel. If the organizers of this symposium believe, as I have the suspicion they do, that presiding over and moderating the session are tasks for someone whose interests are mainly historical, so that he may feel a little bit more detached and dispassionate in his views on what after all is a very controversial subject, I think they are making a mistake. I don't feel detached or dispassionate about the subject of the Common Market. I feel rather involved, both as an economic historian and as an observer of the contemporary scene. I do believe, despite what was said last night by at least one speaker, that the Common Market, the economic unification of Europe, is indeed a bold and noble idea. To be sure, like all bold and noble ideas, it could be somewhat bolder and somewhat nobler. But such as it is, it would be a grievous error to underestimate both what has been achieved so far and what still can and I think what we must hope will be achieved.

Last night it was said that in dealing with the problem of European unification history is really rather unimportant; that we have to treat European unification simply as a contemporary problem. I must disagree with this view. Historically speaking, as I see it, the Common Market with all its spatial and substantive shortcomings, is a radical attempt to continue a process that began centuries ago, with a struggle against medieval localism—when that localism gave way to the economy of organized statehoods. (Incidentally, "nation-state," a term that is used so often, is in my opinion a rather poor term. In some languages "nation" and "state" are synonymous or nearly synonymous. In other languages they are not. Which means that a concept of "nation-state" is either pleonastic, is either redundant, or if it is not redundant is in so many cases historically and also contemporaneously, that is, empirically wrong.) Now this transformation of medieval localism was essentially engineered by what is known as mercantilism. Mercantilism, economically speaking, was an attempt at unification within the boundaries of the individual states, a unification in the interest of economic development. That was unfortunately blurred by what the late Professor Schumpeter once called Adam Smith's unintelligent criticism. As a result, let's say, in the Great Depression of the thirties, whenever a quantitative restriction on trade was imposed or a measure of exchange-control taken, people would always speak of neomercantilism. But both the prefix and the term itself were altogether wrong. Those measures taken during the Great Depression in a period of stagnation and decay had nothing, nothing whatsoever to do with mercantilism, either new or old. The truth is that it was economic liberalism that completed the work of unification which mercantilism began within the individual states, and beyond that did much to reduce the economic significance of political boundaries.

This development was reversed in some respects in the other so-called Great Depression, which began in the 1870's, and it was broken by the First World War. The Common Market of today, as I see it, may be justly and truly viewed as indeed neomercantilism—as an attempt, that is, to continue the job of economic unification in the interest of economic development. Just as laissez-faire completed what mercantilism began, I think the neomercantilism of the Common Market is trying to complete the job of economic liberalism.

I should say that the historical tasks left by the past for the Common Market are great indeed, as the Market is called upon to correct the errors, and perhaps atone for, the sins of that other Great Depression. I am speaking specifically of the agricultural problem that has plagued the Common Market and caused some of the most dramatic moments in that series of crises which have beset the institution. It was in the last quarter of the 19th century that, in France and Italy and above all in Germany, wrong decisions were taken and the crucial moment for adjustment, retrenchment and modernization of agriculture was missed. The result was that elements of what may justly be called a dual economy were preserved until today in the economies of all these countries. Sometime ago I was in Germany, studying the plants, the steel mills, in the Ruhr, and admiring the equipment, the modern technology, the efficiency of the plants. After that I had to go to Hesse, just about a hundred miles away from the Ruhr Valley. When I took a look at the agriculture in this area, I was indeed amazed to see peasants working in small fields, their holdings dispersed over a number of fields, the plow being pulled not indeed by a tractor, and not by a pair of strong horses, but as likely as not by a cow, or sometimes ignominiously a cow and a horse hitched together. You couldn't help being struck by this tremendous contrast between the modernity in the one place and the nearly medieval, if not worse, conditions in the other. It is this duality that the Common Market has to face. Little, I'm afraid, has been done about it so far, and the present system of unified prices plus subsidies, which provides the basis and temporary solution, does not solve the problem. And yet I think that even here, an optimistic view may be justified.

The solution may come through the combined effect of the institutional pressures, rearrangements within the mechanism, within the machinery, of the Common Market, and a sustained high rate of growth. The latter, the high rate of growth, is probably the key to all—or at least to many—of the questions about the Common Market. Growth can be the result of the operation of the Common Market, and at the same time it is also a condition of its success. The promise of a better location of resources, which

37

indeed is implicit in any customs union, can be realized and redeemed only if the rate of growth is high. But it is essentially only the incremental enterprises that we can hope can be located in the most advantageous areas. And it is only a high rate of growth that will allow for the individual plants to reach their optimal size. Even so, the utilization of freedom of factor movements, no doubt so far an actual and positive achievement of the Common Market, will mean much or will mean little depending precisely on how speedily economic development can proceed.

No doubt all this raises very serious problems. The creation of a large area within a customs union has some deleterious effects. What it does, in semi-technical language, is really to convert what is known as comparative cost differences into absolute cost differences. Factor movements can take place, and that can easily mean that in a less advantageous area the factors begin to move out according, so to speak, to their volatility coefficients. First capital moves out, then the entrepreneurs—the most daring, the most venturesome, the better entrepreneurs—move out, and finally labor moves out—again the best elements of labor move out first —and that may lead to a cumulative process of deterioration in a certain area. This may constitute a serious problem; I suppose Signor La Malfa will agree that was precisely what happened in the Italian South.

But on the other hand, there are positive long-term effects of the freedom of labor movements, of labor mobility, over a large area. I think those effects cannot be overestimated. And they do transcend the sphere of economics, raising social problems of great moment and magnitude, because despite its industrial revolutions and despite the economic miracles, Europe still to a very large degree is, if I may call it that, a settled, rather than a migratory society—a settled society burdened with a value system that is not really consonant with the actualities and particularly with the potentialities of a modern economy. When labor mobility fully develops, when it becomes more than just a temporary migration of males, then I think a great step may be taken forward towards economic development and at the same time perhaps also towards the cultural unification of Europe.

I've talked advisedly here about long-run problems and long-run promises, and I know that the short-run problems of course are there. It is perhaps the short-run problems that constitute real dangers. I know, for instance, that power aspirations designed to provide—what shall I say—a *raison d'être,* a justification, a vindication for the political position of one individual, power aspirations which are altogether in the realm of phantasy and unreality, can inflict, unreal and unrealistic as they are, very real damage. I hope, however, that in our discussion we shall hear not only about those short-run problems, but will also not lose sight of what has been accomplished so far and of the promise and the potentialities that the future can bring.

PROF. KINDLEBERGER: French history, as is generally acknowledged, is full of counterpoint. Political scientists say that France varies in its history between the strong man, such as Napoleon, Louis Napoleon, Poincaré and one who is around now, and the so-called "parliamentary game," in which people turn to dividing up the pie rather than trying to expand it. Sometimes the parliamentary game leads to stalemate. Another counterpoint, which interests us today, is the counterpoint between an international outlook and an inward-looking one. I suggest that the international position, that is, an outgoing attitude and thrust to economic policy, can be based upon two kinds of policies and circumstances at home, one that things are going well, and the other that things are not.

France, like every other country in Europe from 1953–4 to 1963–4, was in a period of growth, rapid, successful, dynamic, thrusting growth, which led to a sizeable reallocation of labor, a movement of people off the farm and out of small isolated handicrafts and artisans into bigger firms. This modernization was called in Germany the "wirtschaftswunder," in Italy the "miraculo economico," and of course in France a "miracle économique."

During this period, with everybody pulling in harness and moving rapidly, with rates of growth of 6-8-9 per cent a year, it was possible to turn to constructing Europe. There were the difficulties of 1957–8 in France and the necessity to devalue the currency, but once that was accomplished and everything was back in order with de Gaulle's leadership, policy turned outward again. Then followed a period of growth which lasted five more years.

The crisis came in the fall of 1963, when France, as previously Italy and as later Germany, ran out of extra labor. I place great stress on the contribution of an unlimited supply of labor at the margin to economic growth. Any sector that was growing could bring in new labor and expand—wages were held down, profits were high, and were reinvested. This was a positive feedback growth process, with growth which succeeded by itself. From growth to growth, nothing exceeds like excess, nothing succeeds like success, and so on.

All went well until 1963. First the Italians ran into difficulty. In 1964 the Netherlands' wage system broke down, with an increase of wages in one year of some 20–30 per cent. In France the fateful decision was made in the fall of 1963 to slow down inflation, and if necessary to slow down growth, to abandon or to subvert economic planning, on which it was thought, I think wrongly, that growth had so strongly depended. This decision led to new budgets in September and November '63, and to a slowdown in growth.

The purpose I think was that the French had decided to go for *gloire*. "What Price Gloire?" The price turned out to be high in terms of unrest at home. The independent nuclear deterrent (the *force de frappe*), independent technology, the attempt to resist international corporations, the attempt particularly to play the international big-time monetary game by acquiring gold, holding down prices, having a positive surplus in the balance of payments and thereby acquiring gold—all these were parts of an independent, nationalistic approach to international affairs. You can date it perhaps not from the fall of 1963 but from January

40

of that year when the General said "No" to the British bid for admission into the Common Market. This was about the time when France began pursuing an independent line.

In this period the Common Market took on a rather different kind of tone. Up to then the countries had been growing together, keeping pace with one another. With the end of positive feedback growth, the position became more balanced. One man's growth was another man's recession. This had advantages, but it was not the Common Market as planned. The Common Market was intended to be an economic integral, which would have common policies—fiscal policy, monetary policy, all economic policies moving together. From 1963 on, what happened was that when Italy was inflated, Germany was not, and Italy had a big import surplus, and bought more Volkswagens than I like to think about (certainly than the Fiat company liked to think about). The next year the French were deflated and Italy expanded and these countries balanced each other. This was a benefit that derived from the Common Market, but it was not common policies applied uniformly. In the monetary field there was a stop to integration. Tremendous difficulty was encountered in achieving a common agricultural policy, a difficulty which was acutely political. German farmers were inefficient and the French farmers were gaining efficiency at a rapid rate and needed to get rid of produce. The authorities couldn't move French farmers off the farm into cities fast enough, because they weren't trained and equipped for the city. This meant that as their productivity increased on the farm, they produced more and more butter, wheat and so on. The surpluses thus created are having repercussions on the United States, as well as on Germany.

I should perhaps add parenthetically that long before all this, the Common Market had broken down on the issue of coal. Coal, as you know, is sometimes regarded as underground agriculture. It has the same problems of labor which is not mobile or transferable, doesn't know anything else, is culturally and socially apart from the commonweal, and therefore has to be treated separately.

Coal provided the start of the Common Market back in the Schumann plan of 1950, but this very quickly broke down. The agricultural agreement of 1964–5 just squeaked through by a hair. Further difficulties were reached in agreeing in 1967. Moreover these arrangements are starting to collapse because of national problems which are not internationally harmonized.

Now we come to French unemployment—and to exactly how much unemployment had to do with "les événements de mai-juin," as we call them in the trade (why they're called the events and not the troubles, I don't know). The events of May and June are ascribed by many people in France to unemployment. Unemployment figures, by American standards, look trivial, but the figures are difficult to interpret in these cases. In fact unemployment is rather substantial, particularly in terms of French traditions and French views. More than that, it was concentrated in certain groups, particularly youth, and particularly among university graduates of what might be called the soft social sciences: psychology, sociology, anthropology, and so on, where the activists tend to gather.

There is, by the way, another and a quite different view, that my colleague, Robert Triffin of Yale, for example, would espouse: that les événements de mai-juin had nothing to do at all with unemployment, but were solely a matter of infection from Berkeley, Columbia, the University of Rome, and so on, pure measles run riot, leaping the trivial boundary in ideas based by the Atlantic Ocean. I don't claim to be an expert on these matters, but I would call to your attention the fact that there is an important body of opinion in France which says the unemployment was serious. The trouble started with the revolt of the students, and spread to the revolt of the workers. At this point French policy turned inward toward purely domestic affairs. The *force de frappe,* the policy for all azimuths, the nuclear submarines—all these aspects of *gloire* were slowed down, put off. The Francophone Zone, the policy of glory in the Communauté of Africa, were also stalled, cut down. Attention was turned inward.

If the French had adopted a more active social policy earlier, instead of the policy of glory, they probably would have been able to economize only 2 per cent of national income. Most people think 2 per cent of national income is trivial. It is not, provided it can be massed, focused, invested, and reallocated to the critical sectors. It is true that French education had experienced an enormous expansion, but it wasn't enough and it wasn't of the right kind. Two per cent of national income reallocated to the fields of education and social welfare (particularly more attention to unemployment) might have made a major difference. This last inward-looking phase of French economic life began with the unhappy (to an economist) result of the Accord de Grenelle, that is a 15% wage increase. A wage increase is not the economic answer for unemployment. On the other hand, it may be the only poltical outcome possible. That is the difficulty. One cannot fault the government of last summer for giving this increase, but it created more unemployment. In order to cope with this, the authorities undertook a policy of expansion. This has reversed the contractionary policies, which had been in existence since 1963, a relative contraction embarked upon in order to play the international money game. French leaders turned to expansion and were willing to spend some international reserves, giving up some of their weight in the international monetary game for the sake of a better domestic policy.

But then broke out a different kind of revolt. After the revolt of the students and the revolt of the workers, came the revolt of the middle class. It happened by accident that a piece of legislation that the government had been working on for some years to revise taxes on inheritances came up just at a time when the French undertook an expansionary monetary policy. This policy put money into the system which the middle class decided to take to Switzerland in one form or another, or to convert into gold. This was the strike of the middle class following the strike of the students and the strike of the workers, which constituted the troubles of last November. This led the French into a new kind

43

of confrontation within the Common Market, contemplating squarely the possibility of the devaluation of the franc, but preferring the revaluation upward of the German currency. The Germans, however, have their own "hangups," and particularly an election in September. Mr. Strauss, who is the Finance Minister, is not quite certain that he wants to encounter the wrath of the export interests. Ruhr workers and farmers want to keep the exchange rate the way it is (particularly the farmers for whom, because of the Common Market policies, prices would decline if the currency were revalued).

The confrontation accounts for the Soames episode. It used to be that Germany was the ally of France inside the Common Market, and France didn't need Britain. If Germany gets stronger, and France looks weaker after the events of May and June and the strike of November, France could possibly use another ally inside the Common Market. This would easily account for the beginning of a turn to Britain. Things are going not well internally in France and the country turns abroad to see what it can do in this area.

The Common Market is a political matter primarily because the economic entity that's involved is not the Common Market but a much wider group. We have proof of this all along the line: in GATT the big negotiation is not within the Common Market, but between the Common Market and the United States. In the international corporation, there are no European corporations. The only truly European corporations are American corporations, which are much more European because they feel equally at home in any part of Europe. Fiat is a national monument, as I was told by an Italian once, and de Gaulle thought very long and hard before he was willing to let Fiat and Citröen merge. The only large European merger, across German-Belgian lines between Agfa and Gevaert, is not really a merger—it's not a marriage, it's an arrangement. The two companies are not fully merged but keep two boards of directors, two sets of managers. Only the American corporation has one single decision-making power operating in the Common Market as a whole.

More than that, only one currency operates in the Common Market as a whole, and that's the Eurodollar (the Eurodollar happens to be a dollar which is outside the United States, and that saves it from political overtones). There's only one international capital market, and that's the Eurodollar-bond market, with American corporations in Europe doing most of the borrowing. One could also say that the Common Market as regards labor is mostly again an outside market. It's the Mediterranean workers who are mobile. Frenchmen don't go to Germany very much. A few go across from Strasbourg to Karlsruhe, but mostly the southern Italian, if you'll allow me to call him a Mediterranean and not a Common Market worker for the moment, or the Greek, Turk, Portuguese or Spaniard is prepared to move for extra pay to Germany. He is mobile, whereas the domestic worker is not. American capital is mobile, whereas domestic capital is not. In other words the wider, more competitive far-reaching common market is a common market from which it is very difficult to exclude the United States.

This is why I regard the Six—or the Six plus such allies as they can pick up—as largely a political arrangement, in which it's impossible to effect real symbols of political integration. This could be changed by a couple of acts of heroism, which probably cannot be achieved, one being to unify the monetary systems of the six countries. As I look over economic functions, the really sensitive one, the one which is the saddle point, where countries decide whether they are really politically integrated or not, is money. In 1948 our monetary arrangement with the Russians broke down over whether the eastern zone of Berlin would have the same currency as the three western zones. This produced the blockade, the airlift and the irreversible split of the city.

The other act of heroism is the European statute of incorporation, which people have thought about for a long time but which is getting nowhere fast.

Political integration, or even economic integration on these issues proceeds faster and better within the wider sphere of Europe and North America than it does in the narrower sphere of the Six. The Six by themselves pose political rather than economic issues. The economic issues still ahead over the years, over such questions as agriculture, money, corporations, involve as much the United States and Canada, plus that honorary Atlantic country, Japan, as they do the six countries of the Common Market.

The Present State of the European Economic Community

SIG. LA MALFA: The Treaties of Rome have marked a new road: the road towards integration; they have established a new system: the system of Community institutions; they have introduced a new method: the method of continued and permanent negotiations, aiming at the gradual attainment of determined political and economic objectives, amongst the governments of the signatory countries multilaterally and amongst these same governments and the Community institutions.

The road towards integration has proved to be the right one, because it presupposes a readiness to reach a peaceful collaboration amongst different national states, and because, by means of the enlargement of markets, it allows a greater utilization of our scientific, technical and economic resources in order to improve the living standard of our peoples. This road, which has been followed by the six countries of the European Common Market, is now being taken also by other countries in Europe, in Africa, in Central and South America and in Asia.

The European Community has also proved to be a real stimulant for and a fundamental nucleus of union and peace, and not of division and conflict in Europe. This is clearly proved by the renewed interest of other European countries, especially Great Britain, in entry into the Community, and by the continued development of economic relations between the member countries and Eastern European countries. The Community, moreover, thanks to its increased potential for production and consumption, has greatly facilitated a general expansion of trade, and has brought about a more determined intervention in favor of the developing countries. It has also been the fundamental and

46

inspiring basis for the world tariff negotiations, the "Kennedy Round."

The results which have been achieved by the process of economic integration can be illustrated by use of statistics. During the first ten years of the Common Market (from 1958 to 1967), the gross national product of the six member countries more than doubled, increasing to 340 billion dollars in 1967. Taking into account the effects of price increases, in its first ten years, the Community increased its production 56 per cent. From 1958 to 1967 the general index of the industrial production of the Community also showed a global increase of 67 per cent, which corresponds to an average annual rate of increase of 5.9 per cent.

In addition, trade amongst the member states of the European Community, which in 1958 totalled 6.8 billion dollars, has increased regularly, and in 1967 totalled 24.2 billion dollars. The present volume of Community trade is therefore equivalent to almost four times the volume of 1958 and shows a rate of average annual increase of 15 per cent. Because of this trade, the interdependence of the economies has greatly increased during this period. Whereas in 1958 trade amongst the member countries represented only 30 per cent of the Community's imports and exports, it now is about 45 per cent.

As regards, moreover, trade between the European Economic Community and third countries, in 1967 it totalled 30.8 billion dollars in imports and 31.6 billion dollars in exports. In spite of a decrease of the quota regarding trade with third countries in the total trade of the member countries, which is a natural consequence of the Common Market, the Community's foreign trade has also benefited from its internal expansion, as is evident in the 90 per cent growth in imports and the 100 per cent growth in exports since 1958.

The industrialized Western countries absorb a greater and ever increasing part of this trade: 55 per cent of the imports and 65 per cent of the exports in 1967. They include the most important customers and suppliers of the Community, that is to say the

United States and the United Kingdom, with which trade increased by 100 per cent in imports and by 138 per cent in exports from 1958 to 1967.

As regards the developing countries, among which Latin America has a predominant place, imports have increased much more (69 per cent) than exports (34 per cent). This same evolution characterizes also trade with Madagascar and the African States: an increase of 43 per cent in imports and of 30 per cent in exports.

Italy has surely taken advantage of this economic development: amongst all the member countries, Italy has developed most rapidly. In 1957 the per capita gross national product in Italy was a little more than 600 dollars, whereas the Community average was 950 dollars. This difference was the consequence of a different economic structure: Italy was really the least industrialized country. But, in the period beginning with 1957, the Italian per capita national product increased by 113 per cent, whereas the Community average was only 92 per cent. Also, the contribution of agriculture to the Italian national product fell to 13 per cent, whereas industrial production increased by about 80 per cent. Trade with the EEC countries greatly increased from 1958 to 1967: between 1958 and 1967 Italian imports from the other member countries went from 687 million dollars to 3.390 billion dollars, and exports in the same period went from 608 million dollars to 3.073 billion dollars, the rates of total increase respectively being of 393 per cent and 454 per cent. Also trade with third countries has considerably increased in the same period: imports by more than 50 per cent and exports by more than 170 per cent.

Up to now economic integration has on the whole been accomplished within the timetable set, and in some cases it has even been achieved before the established date. For example, the custom's union was adopted a year and a half before the end of the transition period, which undoubtedly represents a very important step. The abolition of customs barriers within the Community and the free circulation of workers are facts of historic importance. This, however, should not be considered a point of arrival, but only a point of departure, from which to proceed along the road of European integration.

The present moment is crucial. The little time left before the 1st of January, 1970, is the final phase of the transition period. The fundamental distinction between this transition period, and the period of the definitive implementation of the regulations of the Common Market, is that in the first period some national autonomy in fundamental commercial, agricultural, social and industrial policies is still allowed. In the following period these policies should substantially be carried out by the Community, although the classification of steps necessary to proceed from the transition phase to the phase of the definitive implementation of the Community cannot be a rigid one. These steps must be established in an interpretive manner. But it now seems that it will be necessary, at the end of the transition period, to implement the whole of these steps, so as to bring about a true integration of structures in the various economic fields during the following period.

The dynamic development of the economies of the member countries and the present process of economic and social integration have pointed out the necessity of carrying out in the economy of the member countries vast and far-reaching structural reforms. Indeed together with the development of the process of economic integration, together with increased international competitiveness and the utilization of new techniques and new methods of production, it is necessary to undertake a structural policy that will bring about an increased productivity in the economy of the Community and the subsequent strengthening of its international competitiveness. This objective should be carried out during the phase of the definitive implementation of the Common Market. That is to say that during the brief amount of time that we have left, it will be necessary to establish a basis so that later structural reforms can be carried out.

49

Let us then review the main problems that still remain to be solved in each sector.

In the sector of commercial policy, Article 113 of the Rome Treaty provides that at the end of the transition period the commercial policy of the Community should be based on uniform criteria, particularly regarding the stipulation of commercial agreements. It furthermore states that, at the same time, any commercial negotiation with third countries should be carried out by the Commission. The decision adopted by the Council on October 9, 1961 states that on December 31, 1969 all bilateral commercial agreements between the member states and third countries are to expire.

The application of the above-mentioned norms requires as of the 1st of January, 1970, that an accord be reached within the Community regarding the required understandings in the field of a common commercial policy. The knowledge that it will be impossible to reach this accord this year has induced the Commission to draw up a proposal for the Council, providing for the renewal of the commercial agreements now in force and for negotiations for new agreements with third countries. This proposal aims at preparing a common discipline which regulates the renewal of the agreements before the end of the transition phase, and also represents the beginning of commercial negotiations as provided for by Article 113.

The procedure proposed by the Commission could represent a valid solution of the problem insofar as it would establish a common policy for all the member countries in their commercial relations with third countries, and it may constitute a preparatory phase for the subsequent transition to a common commercial policy.

However, there are obstacles as regards both the implementation of Article 113 and the realization of the procedure proposed by the Commission. Direct negotiations between the Commission and third countries are relatively easy where commercial relations with advanced market economy countries or developing countries are involved. But the same cannot be said for those countries having a state-economy: these refuse to recognize the Community and therefore to negotiate with it. In such a situation it would seem advisable that the member countries adopt a common stand, and thus avoid adopting bilateral initiatives which could prejudice the implementation of the procedures regarding the common commercial policy of the Market.

As far as the relationship between the Community and the United States is concerned, it is well known that recently there have been several causes of tension involving reciprocal accusations of protectionism. However, it would be an exaggeration to claim, at least at present, that these differences are serious or unsolvable. What is necessary, nevertheless—and perhaps more on America's part than on Europe's—is that the problem of the relationship between the Community and the United States be re-examined in its entirety, and that this be done systematically, as in the past, with results that were undoubtedly positive. To this end it is fundamental that the pledges made in the Kennedy Round be respected, by doing away with the American Selling Price so as to be able to proceed to the second stage of the planned tariff reductions.

Moreover, it is now necessary for the Market to proceed with more speed towards a real economic union, so as to realize, though with the necessary gradualism, the free circulation of capital, fiscal harmonization and common policies in such important fields as energy and transportation and in the monetary field.

As regards a common agricultural policy, a unified market has been achieved for about 90 per cent of agricultural products. Practically the only products not included are wine and tobacco, which are, however, of great interest to Italy.

However, the establishment of unified prices, often adopted not for economic reasons but as a result of political compromises, even though it has permitted the abolishment of customs barriers and a considerable increase in trade amongst the members of the Common Market, and even though it has contributed to the in-

51

creased income of farmers, thus avoiding social injustice, has proved burdensome to the Community. Moreover, the policy of agricultural price supports has resulted in a serious disparity between the prices for agricultural products within the EEC and the prices prevalent in international trade. This disparity has required the adoption of complicated compensation mechanisms that undoubtedly have had a negative influence on the development of international commerce.

The lack of success of the present system, which, however, has had an important function in the establishment of a unified market for agricultural products, has induced the Commission to face the problem in its entirety, and to view it in terms of structural reform, thus placing agricultural reform within the wider framework of a general economic policy for the development of our Community. The future common agricultural policy, as it has been outlined by the Commission, appears to be a vast system of economic re-equilibrium, by which investments and resources are channeled towards agriculture so as to transform and to adjust it to other economic sectors.

Italy has welcomed this project for the reform of the Community's agricultural structures as submitted by the Commission. Indeed, our country, while cooperating in the establishment of the Common Market for agricultural products, has never ceased to underline on all those occasions when major decisions were adopted in this field, that emphasis should have been placed by the Community on structural reform.

The proposal for the reform of agricultural structures will surely, if it is realized, have important effects on commercial relations with third countries. This aspect of the proposal is important to Italy, which is an exporter of agricultural products. In the first ten years of Community life, we have observed that the gradual implementation of a common agricultural policy has exerted a great influence on the quantity and on the type of the agricultural trade between the Community and third countries: in particular with the Eastern European countries, the Latin America countries and the developing countries in general. In reforming the Community's agricultural structures, we must carefully consider this aspect, for its political consequences are quite important, and it is also clearly connected with the problem of the elimination of surpluses both as regards over-production and undernourishment in the world.

The difficult task which the Community must carry out in this sector during 1969 is the following: on the one hand we must complete a common agricultural policy, while maintaining an adequate equilibrium between the interests of the member countries, and on the other hand we must establish the basis for a policy regarding agricultural structures to be carried out during the period of the definitive implementation of the Common Market.

Another important problem is that the establishment of the customs union has not entirely eliminated obstacles which hinder Community trade. There are still serious impediments caused by the differences in fiscal legislation. Although results in this sector are as yet not very conspicuous, careful studies are being made in all branches of taxation that should lead to concrete solutions.

In the social field, the Community has achieved outstanding results in several sectors. I think particularly of those sectors where the objectives to be reached were outlined in detail by precise provisions of the Rome Treaty, especially those concerning the free circulation of workers, the establishment and free exercise of services, and also, despite the difficulties that are being encountered in the discussions, the revision of the current regulations concerning the social security of migrant workers.

On the other hand, in other sectors, the Community has had greater difficulty in outlining its course of action. In fact, there has been a real lack of progress in achieving the general objectives established by the Treaty in matters of social policy, particularly in the sectors of employment, professional training, and the standardization of social legislation.

The activity of the European Social Fund, which was conceived as one of the Community's financial instruments for intervention in the social field, should have had a determining effect in the social policy of the Community. However, it has not managed substantially to affect the employment and professional training policies of the member countries.

At every possible opportunity, Italy has always sought to broaden Community action in social matters by taking the initiative and supporting progressive solutions tending to give the Commission broader powers. However, this action has not achieved the desired concrete results, except in the various sectors concerning the free circulation of individuals.

Under the present circumstances, then, the most realistic solution for broadening the social activities of the Community seems to be that of aiming for an adequate strengthening of the European Social Fund through reorganization. This is explicitly provided for by the Treaty itself, to take effect at the beginning of the definitive period.

The results of European economic integration have also been modest in the industrial sector. This becomes even more serious if one considers that the interdependent relationship resulting from the progressive achievements of the Common Market has come to mean that every governmental intervention in the economy of a country or of a region inevitably has repercussions on the economy of the other member countries, and thus on the competitive capacity of each of them and of the Community as a whole. In fact, each member country still retains more or less complete autonomy to influence the productive conditions of the enterprises in its own territory. These interventions are carried out without an overall plan and without taking into consideration their repercussions on the interests of the Community. They should, instead, be coordinated and in keeping with our common objectives.

However, it should not be forgotten that by adopting the second program of the medium-range economic policy, the member countries have pledged themselves to take into consideration, when establishing their national economic policies, the guidelines contained in that document. These emphasize the need for encouraging and carrying out structural changes and of doing so in a manner compatible with our common industrial objectives. This therefore is a very important step towards defining and achieving a common policy for industrial structures.

The problems dealt with thus far, which might generally be defined as problems concerning the internal development of the Community, are so complicated and so important that they cannot be considered separately nor isolated from the general political context in which the Community exists and acts. In fact, it is not permissible, and on this point the Italian position has always been extremely clear, for European governments and peoples to involve themselves in such historically important activities, without being aware and without having an exact idea of the historical, geographical, economic and political dimensions of the European continent. Therefore, the problem of the internal development of the Community is inseparable from that of its external expansion.

As far as the fundamental political problem of the relationship between the Community's internal development and its external expansion is concerned, it should be pointed out that the latter must not entirely condition the former, much less hinder it. Indeed it should be acknowledged that priority must be given to the internal development of the Community, which forms the nucleus for an irreversible process towards the political and economic integration of Europe. However, not a single step should be taken towards the internal development and the economic integration of the Six, without considering at the same time the impact of each step and new achievement on the relationship between the Community and countries that are candidates for membership. Moreover, it is the very impetus of the Community and the problems on the agenda at Brussels which continue to emphasize the inadequacy of the present institutional organization of the Community, the inadequacy of its geographic and productive dimensions and the impossibility of proceeding on an economic and commercial level without creating a political unity. This situation offers those member countries in favor of the entry of Great Britain the possibility of carrying on Community activities that constantly emphasize the relationships between a strengthened and an expanded Community and between an economic and a political Europe.

On the external level, the member countries interested in expansion—within limits that assure the continued existence of the Community, and without going beyond the breaking point—continue to follow the line of action established at the beginning of 1968. That is, they follow the policy of taking all possible political and economic initiatives (political collaboration, technical and industrial cooperation, etc.) aimed at achieving on a bilateral—and preferably a multilateral—level even partial or limited advances towards the geographic expansion of the Community and the political unification of Europe.

On the other hand there are no real alternatives to complete and unconditional membership of countries that have not yet applied for entry into the Community. There is no alternative to the expansion of the present institutional structure. The mere creation of a free trade area between the Community and countries that are candidates for membership is not a realistic and concrete possibility. In today's world the abolition of customs barriers is no longer sufficient to give new impetus to individual economies, because the tariff factor has lost importance in international exchange regulations. We see this by observing that England, Denmark and Norway already are part of a free trade area involving other European countries, but the benefits that they have been able to gain from it have been relatively minor and seem now to be at an end.

The problem of completing and strengthening the institutions of the Community are of a strictly political nature and are inseparably connected to the Communty's expansion. The establishment of a system for electing a European Parliament by direct universal suffrage is of particular importance and great urgency. In fact, although what has been accomplished up to now in the Community is the result of an equilibrium reached on a governmental level, this system is no longer adequate for the future. The relationship between the people of Europe and the Community institutions can no longer be an entirely indirect relationship as it has been until now. A real agricultural, commercial, industrial and social policy presupposes that the European population speaks directly through the voice of chosen representatives.

Finally, as is explicitly sanctioned in the Rome Treaty, it is necessary that the Community have its own resources to ensure sufficient autonomy, and to give it the possibility of acting as a stabilizing force in certain critical sectors.

In concluding our economic analysis, we thus see that the EEC was conceived as a fundamental nucleus for the political and economic unification of Europe, as a valid instrument for the general expansion of trade, in solidarity with the developing countries, and as a force for "détente" in the world.

The association status of Greece and Turkey, of the African countries and Madagascar, of Nigeria, Kenya, Tanzania, Uganda, the existing commercial agreements with Lebanon, with Iran and Israel, the partial agreements signed recently with Morocco and Tunisia, in view of their future association status, the major role played by the Community during the Kennedy Round negotiations, the recent offer by the Community at the OECD to extend general preferences to industrial products and to agricultural products (agricultural food products) imported from developing countries, demonstrate by substantial achievements that the European Community is able to pursue those aims and that it is faithful to the ideals and principles which inspired it.

For these reasons, it must be open to other European Countries; for these same reasons its internal structure can not allow for the existence of retrogressive and divisive nationalisms. This is why its institutions must be strengthened, and above all why it is urgent to begin the process leading to political integration, with the participation of the United Kingdom necessary as soon as possible.

The solution of the problem of a divided Germany, the establishment of a more balanced and more solid basis for the relationship between Europe and the United States, and between Europe, the Soviet Union and the Communist world, and between Europe and the developing countries, can only be brought about by an enlarged European Economic Community—a Community on its way to becoming a political community founded on a democratic basis, which will be a pillar of peace and progress in the world.

Political Considerations

The advantages deriving from the organization of economic activity, not within the framework of the traditional national spaces in Europe, but over a large continental space, have been demonstrated, in a most impressive way, by the results achieved by the Common Market. We have outlined these achievements in the first part of this report. Before this important experience there was a great impulse towards European unity, determined by predominantly political reasons. And the experience of the Common Market has given this impulse formidable support in an exclusively economic sense. Without the Common Market, the development of reciprocal exchanges among the Six from 6,790 million dollars in 1958 to 24,161 millions in 1967 would have been impossible.

Of course, during this time, there have been instances of standstill, of a slowing down of the development of inter-exchange, determined by internal economic unbalance in this or that country, and above all by deficits in the balance of payments. Nevertheless, the rhythm of increase has been maintained—as we have seen—at an exceptionally high level.

The paradox of the situation lies, however, in the fact that while originally political reasons for integration were easily predominant but were not borne out by concrete economic experience, today when this economic experience has been gained (fairly positively) the political reasons, which called for a speeded-up process of European unification, are now a subject of serious discussion.

58

This is but one of the many aspects of the present crisis in Western Europe, which takes a place of its own beside the far more serious crisis of Eastern Europe.

The political reasons which after the Second World War led to a powerful movement for the creation of a European state of a federal type (that is, the creation of a European continental political power, side by side with the big political powers today represented by the United States of America and by the Soviet Union), have been challenged in recent years—as is known—by the France of de Gaulle. France, while accepting the experience of the Common Market, has not chosen to draw the logical consequence from such an acceptance, namely, the creation of a federal political organization, within which the Common Market could have developed further. Instead, de Gaulle's France has chosen to interpret the Common Market as the simple outcome, in the economic field, of a collaboration between entirely traditional sovereign states, that is, states not obliged to give up any part whatsoever of their sovereignty. In other words, while the Common Market, in the opinion of important European political currents, should have been the anticipation in economic terms of a federal Europe more or less similar in its development to the United States of America, General de Gaulle chose to make it the simple product of a Europe of individual and entirely sovereign states.

A first crisis, in present-day Europe, stems from this differing evaluation of the manner of conceiving of the European unit. And this is a crisis which opposes de Gaulle's France to the federalist aspirations repeatedly expressed by the governments and political forces of the other five countries of the Common Market, and also divides the French themselves.

The second crisis, in present-day Europe, is a direct outcome of the first, and concerns the entry of Great Britain into the Common Market. As long as there existed a real and unquestioned federalist trend in the six countries which then constituted the Common Market, Great Britain, repeatedly invited to take part in such movement, appeared skeptical as to its results. Later, when Great Britain became convinced that the road to economic progress and political strength led through the Common Market and other European organizations, she no longer found the previous favorable situation. Instead the British encountered the purely national, not to say hegemonic, concept of General de Gaulle. This has posed a very strong obstacle to the necessary rapid integration of Europe. France has put forward some non-political motivations for vetoing the British entry; and it was specifically to examine in concrete terms the importance of these motives that the Monnet Committee for the United States of Europe, in the course of its latest meeting in London (March 11), decided to entrust to a number of experts (Guido Carli for the monetary side, Walter Hallstein for institutions, Edgardo Pisani for agriculture, Lord Plowden, Karl Wineradler for tecchnological development) the tasks of referring to the Committee various proposals. But I think the French objections are substantially political and nothing but political. France's exclusive determination and veto have, of course, not been favorably received by the other five countries of the Common Market, who consider Great Britain's entry as useful and necessary. But the Rome Treaty did not give value to anything but unanimous votes. Meanwhile, Great Britain and the other five countries can undoubtedly find a means of political collaboration through the WEU (Western European Union), which they are now doing, despite French protests. But this is not equivalent to British entry into the Common Market, and thus cannot ensure the integration of the British economy into the European continental economy.

It is difficult to foresee how, at the present time, we can get out of this situation which makes Europe waste time—time which is precious with regard to the political and economic problems knocking at its door (and the doors of the rest of the world).

In the meantime, although France's position is based on political reasons, de Gaulle claims to want to preserve the Common Market against any possible negative consequences. In fact, however, considerable negative consequences are already becoming apparent, as we noted in the first part of the report, even in the economic area of the Common Market, slowing it down and weakening its initiatives. Only a few days ago we learned that the Common Market Commission is undecided whether to declare, at the end of the year, the passing—as foreseen by the Rome Treaties—from the "transitory phase" to the "final period." In other words, since the implementation of the economic union is still quite far from being completely achieved, and the uncertainty of the political situation is dependent on the economic, the Commission wonders if it would not be advisable to prolong the "transitory phase" for two or three more years.

Those on the Commission who are in favor of a prorogation of the "transitory phase" consider that, for public opinion, the passing to the "final period" would mean that the fundamental problems have been settled. But I think this is not the case, since we have to allow for long and difficult negotiations on the new "Mansholt plan" for agriculture, and, above all, for its financing. Moreover, the prolongation of the transitory phase would make it possible to establish for the next three years a calendar of precise deadlines for other important problems, such as the strengthening and co-ordination of the current economic and monetary policy of the member states, the working out of a common trade policy, the defining of new pluri-annual programs of research, and the implementation of scientific and technological co-operation. Lastly, by proclaiming the passage to the "final period" at the end of this year, it would no longer be possible to have recourse to the so-called "safeguarding clause" foreseen by Article 226 of the Treaty, for the purpose of protecting the interests of this or that branch of the national economy threatened by the opening of the frontiers.

For their part, the representatives who oppose the prorogation of the "transitory phase" point out that, while in the past the Commission has tried to cover ground rapidly, it would be a serious mistake if we now reached a deadlock. An immediate decision, they claim, would do away with the impression of a serious crisis, resulting from the question of the British entry into the Common Market. Moreover, the passing on to the "final period" would give the common institutions (Council of Members, and Commissions), at the end of the Treaty, new juridical means to speed up the advance towards complete economic union.

It appears that the Commission will decide on this important point immediately after the Easter holidays. However, all this uncertainty reflects a political situation which is very difficult to analyze. The Common Market needs a political frame, and this must necessarily be of a federal nature. Great Britain, while it has previously been hostile to any entry into a European organization which implies a federal bond, did (during the meeting of the Monnet Committee in London, to which I referred, and at which for the first time the representatives of the three British parties played a role) accept a federal tie. Only de Gaulle's France is now hostile to such a tie, continuing to insist on a Europe of individual countries.

It is the almost unanimous opinion of Europeans, including a large part of French public opinion, that Europe cannot be built politically and cannot go forward in the economic field without the introduction—as gradual as this may be—of federal commitments. In fact, two recent books by French authors, which have proved highly successful and which I had the honor of presenting in Italy, stated this need. One is entitled "Le Défi Américain," and is by the authoritative writer and publicist, Servan-Schreiber, and the other is entitled "Le Pari Européen," and is written by technical and other experts such as Louis Armand (formerly of Euratom) and Michel Drancourt.

"The two conditions necessary for an efficient European organization are, first," writes Servan-Schreiber, "authority in certain areas over the individual nation-states, and, second, its own financial resources so that it can carry out large-scale projects that have been jointly agreed upon." Louis Armand on his part, maintains that:

"In order to have a role, Europe too should federate. This is absolutely vital. This needs place it in a vanguard position since humanity cannot jump this stage in its evolution. America need not imagine some type of federation excelling its own. Neither need the USSR. It is Europe which must give the example, and it is time that it does so. These are the only ideas capable, consciously or unconsciously, of truly inspiring young people; and the only ones which, if put into action, will reduce the serious risks facing the world at the dawn of the planetary age."

The battle for Europe is at this juncture. What is required now is an act of courage and political farsightedness by governments and peoples. Without this act, the Common Market, a predominantly economic construction, runs the risk of not forging ahead, and even of falling back. Without this act of courage, not only will Europe not achieve the levels of the new technological civilization, which calls for large spaces, but it will simply be a series of countries, divided and squabbling between themselves, a reproduction between the United States of America and the Soviet Union of the Balkan situation existing between the big European powers prior to the outbreak of the First World War.

DR. THORP: The Nineteen-thirties saw the economies of Europe and United States in deep economic trouble, with uncoordinated national efforts dealing unsuccessfully with widespread unemployment and falling prices, and with the international economy deranged by rapidly rising import barriers, devaluations, and defaults on international payments. The Nineteen-forties were dominated by war destruction and the beginnings of post-war reconstruction. The Fifties saw incredible progress in production and employment, and the exciting growth of new institutions for international cooperation. This happy state of affairs carried over into the Sixties—but more recently, one senses the emergence of a questioning, a doubt, a growing sense of impatience and frustration.

The burdensome defense problem is still uncomfortably with us, accentuated by uncertainty about the future of NATO. The hoped for East-West bridge-building based on the belief that the monolith was crumbling was badly shaken by the Czechoslovak happening. The reuniting of Germany is as far away as ever. Britain is becalmed. France is not even superficially at peace with herself. And frequent financial crises have shaken the financial world. From the European point of view, the extent of dependence on the United States not only for security but even for political leadership is much too great, the technological gap is depressing, and there is no clear common path to follow to unify the separate nations of Europe. From the American side, Europe is still politically fragmented. It is unduly costly in terms of American dollars. It does not appreciate how much we have done for it. And, anyhow, any foreign involvement is a nuisance which distracts the country from the monumental tasks at home.

Perhaps this is the normal psychological reaction which occurs when a set of unreasonably high expectations is deflated by the persistence of problems and the slow pace of progress. We find it difficult to believe that problems are not easily solved. (Our childhood training in arithmetic mistrained us, for there we were given only problems with answers. It was not impressed upon us that one cannot find the exact numerical value of pi, or what is two times infinity.)

This unsatisfactory state of mind is inextricably bound up with various uncertainties about the Common Market. The leading star of a United Europe has undoubtedly dimmed. But has it disappeared? Hereafter I shall focus my remarks more narrowly around four crucial questions relating to European unity:

1) Is the progress of the Common Market coming to a halt?
2) Is the Common Market likely to add to its membership?
3) Will the economic union become a political union?
4) What should be the policy of the United States towards the Common Market?

Question #1. Is the Common Market in a state of stagnation? My answer is that it has made remarkable progress in its relatively short life—and that it is still in the stage of active development.

The original actions which were to establish a common market included the destruction of the boundaries among members as they related to the movement of goods, people, and capital; to the unrestricted establishment of enterprises and the transfer of services; the development of common policies for agriculture, for transport, for foreign trade, for the enforcement of competition and for various social matters; and finally the harmonization of the fiscal structures of the Six and the development of common programs for economic stability.

In many of these fields, progress is far advanced. Tariff barriers have disappeared and labor mobility is virtually complete. The freedom of establishment of new enterprises is largely accomplished, except in a few special fields like insurance and banking. The transfer of services is still not unrestricted in those organized professions which view a limited supply as an important influence on price; the flow of capital is relatively free except in time of crisis. (That's quite frequent.)

In all these fields, there are still many small intransigent areas. Thus, while tariffs have disappeared, certain other obstacles to the free flow of goods still remain. For example, consider the problem of establishing a common market in pharmaceutical products. Each country has regulations relative to particular medicines and drugs, presumably in the interest of the health of its citizens but not disregarding the interest of each country's drug industry. The problem is not one of unequal tariffs but of regulatory barriers. A directive aimed at establishing a common policy with respect to pharmaceutical products was passed by the Council of Ministers in January, 1965. Two years later, only Belgium had taken the appropriate action. France and Italy at least had made gestures of recognition, but Germany, the Netherlands and Luxembourg, as reported in French, *n'ont pas bougé*. The subject is still on the Community's agenda, but nationalism seems to put more stress on where medicines are made than on efforts to improve their quality, availability, or lower the cost.

65

As to common policies, perhaps the greatest achievement thus far is in the field of agriculture. A most intricate agreement involving price supports, protection, subsidies, and a program of structural change all together involving expenditures of well over $2 billion per year, is an economist's nightmare—but agriculture has long been a problem taken over by the politicians. The conflicting interests of the Six have somehow been overcome—and the monstrous result has within itself the possibility of eventually easing the problem. Imagine the political cleverness of providing generous retirement for farmers at age 55, thus delighting them while presumably making it possible to eliminate some of the small, high-cost farms; or at least, opening up farming to a younger generation more familiar with modern farm methods. To be sure, the financing of the program is only on a temporary basis. A permanent formula still has to be agreed upon for what promises to be a rapidly increasing cost.

I must also note the extraordinary development in the fiscal field whereby all of the Six have incorporated the value-added formula in their tax systems, economic institutions which do not yield easily to change as American experience demonstrates. To be sure, the Six are not starting with equal rates but the tax pattern will be the same. This is an important step towards creating a more uniform basis for trade and competition within the Market.

I could go on pointing out how much has been done in the transport field, although rates and relative subsidies remain to be acted upon; how the regulation of competition has been proceeding case by case in slow respectable legal fashion; how the date for terminating national trade monopolies, such as the French monopoly system for imports of petroleum, has been set; how women have been accorded equal pay; how common standards for working conditions such as maximum hours of labor are gradually emerging; and what progress has been made towards the adoption of similar safety rules for automobiles and electrical appliances. However, it is not my intention to present a detailed history but merely to indicate how unbelievably complicated it is to bring six countries with long backgrounds of separate economic and social development into harmony, how much has been done, and how much is in process.

There are three additional problems which I must note briefly that are building up such a head of steam that they may force the Six into new areas of common action: the technology gap, the American corporate invasion, and the recurring crises in the financial field.

While we still think of invention as the product of an imaginative individual at his own work-bench, this is not the way most research is done today. Research is an organized effort involving men and money. Expenditures by the Government, the large corporations, and the universities have given the United States a technological lead in many products and processes. While the extent of the so-called technological gap is probably exaggerated, it has become a matter of general concern in Europe. And back of Western Europe is Eastern Europe with an even greater feeling of inferiority.

A report bearing on technology was due in Brussels in March. So far, I am not aware of much European technological co-operation except in the supersonic plane and the atomic energy fields, and even here the record is disappointing. The problem for Europe is in large part one of resources and of scale. Somehow, individual units, public and private, must find partners to carry the costs and to bring together the essential critical mass of brainpower. European enterprise consists largely of small companies, with dozens of them involved in the making of a product like refrigerators, for example. There still seems to be resistance to mergers which cross national boundaries and which might create a "European" enterprise, and only a very small number of existing multinational enterprises could be so denominated.

The creation of a situation more conducive to research must start with the changing of basic priorities, so that much greater resources of brains and money will be devoted to the world of technology. It would appear to be quite possible to affect the situation by removing barriers and introducing incentives in various forms. At the moment, however, I would have to describe this problem as being in the stage of warming up. It may be that the Common Market will soon move it into the area of action.

Another new problem which I believe has been blown up far beyond its real importance is the charge that American companies are setting up such important beachheads in Europe that they endanger Europe's very independence. The problem, if it is one, is directly traceable to the Market itself. That many American enterprises should shift from trying to surmount the external tariff barriers to producing inside the market seems almost an inevitable consequence.

We assume that the American "invasion" is a good thing. American businessmen enter the Common Market because they believe that they can do a better job than is being done, bringing their modern technology, marketing knowledge, and management skill. This in turn has its impact on the whole level of productivity of other enterprises. As to any challenge to sovereignty, American business would be even less successful in influencing national policy abroad than in the United States. And here, in our pluralistic society, it is one voice among many. If complaints are any index, business regards the United States Government as extremely hard of hearing.

American investment in Europe had a period of boom proportions which is bound to taper off, and the benefits to European economic operation are beginning to appear. If the Common Market must become seized with this problem, I trust that it will recognize the costs involved if barriers are established to the free inflow of management skills and knowledge.

A third problem with fresh emphasis is that of balance-of-payments adjustment, particularly as among the Six. The United States, though in international difficulty, has no adjustment problem among its parts, but the Common Market clearly is not an economic union. While it does publish statistics as to its total payments and reserve position, this is the sum of quite disparate parts rather than of a single economic entity. Since the Common Market operation is based on separate currencies, the operation of an efficient allocation of resources must rest on the assumption of fixed exchange rates and fairly similar price trends.

Programs like that for agriculture, with its substantial flow of funds for price supports and structural change, are stated in dollars. The relative cost-benefit positions of the members would change drastically if either price level trends varied greatly or currencies were re- or de-valued. Thus, the contrary behavior of the German and French financial positions in 1968 makes very clear new directions in which the Six must move. This inevitably involves much closer budgetary and monetary co-operation. The Rome Treaty has a rather vague reference to commitments for "mutual support." Already, it has been proposed that each country discuss its annual budget estimates with the other members, and that part of the reserves of each be earmarked as a common defense fund for mutual assistance in case of trouble. But a single currency for all still seems far away.

After this long listing of old and new problems calling for attention, one might say that there is so long an agenda that it might lead to a sense of helplessness and hopelessness. Not so. The Executive Commission of the Community is clearly pushing for continued progress. In fact, it has presented a program to the Council of Ministers which calls for major steps towards a common monetary and economic policy to be achieved in 1969, and by 1972 for a commercial policy, the reform of the structure of agriculture, and the reduction of the diversity of European social funds. In addition, it regards as immediate Community problems the areas of technological research and of more permanent agricultural financing. It is the recognition of the existence of problems like these which makes certain that the Common Market will not stagnate. Its kind of progress may not provide many headlines, but I am confident that there will be many one-inch and two-inch stories in the press, each of which will represent one more triumph for the Community in its march towards a closer economic union.

Question #2. Will other countries, notably the United Kingdom, become full members of the Community? It is very easy to answer, "No," not only because of General de Gaulle's firm opposition but because time seems to be working in the opposite direction. The initial goal agreed on in Rome was to create a customs union which distinguished between trade within the area and trade outside. However, the outside barrier is also being lowered as provided in the Kennedy Round. Consequently, the trade benefits of being within the customs union are being reduced and the desired economies of scale can be achieved in a freer world trading framework. Sooner or later, there will be still another global tariff-cutting negotiation (I am unable to label it with any Presidential name) and that will make the customs union aspect of the Common Market even less attractive. To a considerable extent, these matters are being handled elsewhere—in GATT, the Committee of Ten, and the OECD.

Not only do the economic arrangements promise to be less and less rewarding, but the initiation fee grows higher and higher. I refer to the intricate process of harmonization—national adjustments in economic, fiscal, and social practices which have been intended to reduce the differences in the separate economic environments. These have occurred gradually and only after careful study of how to minimize the problems created for each member. However, for a new member, this mass of limited, piecemeal adjustments would add up to substantial change to be done rapidly and without modification for the special case. Unless the new member goes through this process, the basic assumption of commonality will fail.

It is not the final answer to say that it will not happen because the economic advantages are lessening and the requirements for membership are growing more arduous. History is not writ only in economic terms, although certain groupings or mergers of nations in the past have been to a considerable degree reactions to the industrial revolution and the need for larger aggregates. Thus Toynbee emphasized the economic in describing the breakdown of French provincial barriers, the unification of the German Länder, and later of the Italian city-states. One might add to the list the increased federalization of the United States.

More often, the immediate cause of past integrations has been military conquest or defense requirements. But in view of the existence of NATO, I doubt if anyone would put forward the need for increased security as a justification for expanding the Community.

One purpose does remain which may prevail over the cost-benefit calculus, so that one cannot answer the question with an unqualified "No." That is the concept of Europe as a third (or perhaps fourth or fifth) power in the world. George Brown, recently unfolding a proposal to launch fresh negotiations for a European Political Community, made this point when he pointed out that, because the concept of uniting the national fragments of Europe was still unachieved, Europe had not been able to exert its united weight in the Czech affair, in the Middle East chaos, in the monetary crises, or in the NATO decisions. Just what a united Europe might have done with these disorderly happenings, he did not say. He really was calling for a Europe with prestige and power built on size.

If one thinks of Britain as no longer with Empire, except perhaps Anguilla, and seeking a new identity while painfully cutting back her far-flung commitments; if one thinks of the Six as including two especially large members without a third whose addition would tend to keep each of the three in its place; if one considers the need for focused enthusiasm in this disorderly world and the appeal to the younger generation of the concept of a united Europe; and if one recognizes that the relationship between size and influence in foreign relations would redound to the *grandeur* of the seven, eight, or more countries involved, then added membership is possible. I would not say that it is probable.

It would require a new leader or a major event or both to bring it about.

Having said all this about the Community, I must add that I am certain that there will be a further development of European institutions and European co-operation. Even though the Organization for Economic Cooperation and Development (OECD) includes the United States, Canada, and Japan among its members, it is primarily a European organization. And here there are consultations on a wide variety of fronts from economic stabilization to the training, recruitment, and utilization of teachers, from border tax adjustments to the prevention of accidents on the highways. In the last month, the Common Market ministers approved a plan for a single patent registration to cover the Six and invited seven other countries, including the United Kingdom, to join in the program. Furthermore, the multi-national companies are providing another force which tends to break down European barriers. Thus Europe can and will become more unified even without added membership in the Common Market.

Question #3. Will the economic union become a political union? If one means—will the Six accept a common supernational government in the near future, I must answer, "No." This is not merely a recognition of General de Gaulle's position, but rather of that intangible but powerful force called nationalism. No one of the Six would agree to give up its so-called sovereignty if the question were put in such black and white terms. However, I would argue that the Six are already well on the way towards political unity. Every step reducing barriers among them in the interest of the total Community is a diminution of national sovereignty.

In 1926, celebrating jointly the one hundred and fiftieth anniversary of the American Declaration of Independence and the publication of *The Wealth of Nations,* Carl Becker spoke at ceremonies at the Brookings Institution. He related a delightful fable about a Dutchman in New York, a strong supporter of the King, whose position changed bit by bit, almost imperceptibly, as provocative events occurred, until finally he found himself a revolutionist. He would never have made the shift in a single jump—but he arrived as the result of a series of small steps which never raised the big issue. It seems to me that this is what is taking place in the Community. Of course, forward motion runs into obstacles. Even within countries, political cement is not unbreakable as the many civil wars in history make clear. National pressures appear in the Community just as regional pressures appear in single states. But the development of common institutions, the taking of joint action in many fields, and the conscious effort to consult and to co-operate—these are political acts reducing national independence of action whether they are dealing with economic, social, or security matters.

The Rome Treaty was not merely an economic and social instrument. By requiring the Six to agree on a common external tariff, it established the interest of the Community as controlling with respect to the political problem of protection, a subject which had heretofore always been managed in terms of each member's national interest. And the agricultural scheme bringing the farmers of all Six within a single frame is an extraordinary political achievement. Again, the agreement embodied in the Convention of Yaoundé with respect to trade and aid with some eighteen former colonies plus four additional "limited-association" states represents a political consolidation in the field of foreign relations.

I do not wish to press this point too far. The European Economic Community is far from being a full-fledged political union. But I do insist that it has considerably reduced the significance of the boundaries among the Six and that many problems formerly handled separately by the Members are now subject to overall action in the Community. Furthermore, this reaches far beyond the formal Community actions of record. For example, before the 1968 Annual Meetings of the International Monetary Fund and the International Bank, the appropriate representatives of the Treasuries and Central Banks in the six countries met to discuss together the various agenda items. So, to sum up the answer to

Question #3, the European Economic Community is moving forward on problem after problem. And as it does so, it chips away at national sovereignties, establishing more and more political unity if not a political union.

Question #4. What should be the policy of the United States towards the Common Market? Perhaps the most important point is to realize that there are substantial limitations on what we can do with respect to the structure of Europe. It is their house which is being built. We are not the builders. We are not the architect. We are interested neighbors, concerned with the character and quality of the neighborhood, willing to be helpful but rather fearful of creating resentments from undue interference with the affairs of others.

It was not always so. In the late Forties, when the United States was deeply involved directly in European affairs, it strongly supported the European group calling for integration, people like Count Sforza, Winston Churchill, Jean Monnet, and Robert Schuman. Initially, this was not an easy decision even for the United States. On the one side were the economists who argued for global, most-favored-nation economic policies. They feared the creation of a sheltered, high-cost area in Western Europe, forced because of its isolation to discriminate more and more against the outside world. And within the area, it was feared that all members would be held back to the economic pace of the slowest.

On the other side were the political experts who viewed the primary problem as the preservation of the peace. They talked of the dangers inherent in any condition of Balkanization, though the term is not a very good description of Western Europe. But their particular concern was the future of West Germany. They were determined that the source of two World Wars should not be in a position once again to call out the engines of war. Therefore, the prospect of a more united Western Europe with Western Germany as a charter member was regarded as a prime objective.

The European Economy: Prospects for Unity?

The political experts won, and fortunately the dire forecasts of the economists were not realized. Economic competitiveness increased within the Common Market area. The unanticipated addition of body-building vitamins in the form of American enterprise enhanced the pace of growth. And instead of added requirements for protection, the Community became more able and willing to liberalize its external relations.

I see no reason for changing the American position as it then developed. We would like to see a strong integrated Europe. We would like to see the Common Market strengthened by the addition of Great Britain. We would like to see the ties grow steadily closer, particularly so that West Germany, with her size and growing economic strength, will feel more certain that her brightest future lies in the growth and development of Western Europe.

This American interest in the unity of Western Europe was vigorously stated by General Eisenhower as long ago as 1951 before the English Speaking Union in London. While he never defined organizationally or geographically what he meant by European unity or integration, he was emphatic that patchwork territorial fences would only pyramid costs and bar the efficient division of labor. In the political field, these barriers would promote distrust and suspicion. And the handicaps of enforced division would make difficult even the minimum essential security effort. On the other hand, he was as lyrical as an Army officer can be in declaring that a united Europe would be a strong Europe which could produce miracles for the common good.

Let me immediately repeat that the United States cannot bring this miracle about. We probably ought not to take too active an interest or we may be counter-productive, as was Secretary Dulles when he made impossible the development of a European Army by threatening his "agonizing reappraisal." Too many of us, including public officials and especially legislators, seem to have a compulsion to make hortatory public comment. What is needed is not so much that we speak more softly but rather less often.

Of course, the situation is complicated by the army of private professional analysts who are prepared to extrapolate any casual comment into a declaration of high policy.

Even though American policy should be relatively quiet, it should have its hopes clearly in mind, avoiding so far as possible actions in other contexts which might interfere with further progress towards European unity. We have many areas where we are both deeply involved and where we are eager for a strong Europe to share world responsibilities with us. One can hope that as the process of integration proceeds, the weight of its internal problems will lessen and Europe can give more attention to the world outside.

We have basic interests in common beyond the exchange of goods, persons, and capital. In the security area we feel that Europe is leaving the problem more and more to us. With respect to aid to less-developed countries Europe feels with considerable justification that we are doing much less than our share. The security of nations from military annihilation and the accelerated economic, social, and political development of the poor countries —these are supreme tasks in which all must share. A more united Europe would make possible a much more effective partnership in working towards a better world.

PROF. GERSCHENKRON: Let me ask a couple of related questions of Professor Kindleberger.

I couldn't help being impressed by his forceful presentation of the case, but I wonder how much emphasis we should really place on de Gaulle. I'm sure that de Gaulle has inflicted a considerable damage, and can inflict perhaps an even greater damage on the Common Market and the European Community, particularly before that fateful date of December 31, 1969. At the same time it is rather understandable why de Gaulle acts the way he does— I don't think it is just a whim of the man or his character. France of course is not a dictatorship, but the paradoxical thing is that de Gaulle has to act as a dictator to provide the justification for his existence by trying to establish what I call the stability conditions of power exercise. That's why he is going on, creating enemies, stirring up troubles with what Professor Thorp just called casual comments or casual remarks—like his casual comment in Quebec. That's why he has to rely on plebiscites. That's why he has to play up that illusive thing called charisma. That is also why he has been unable, like most dictators, to take care of a proper succession. And by that I don't mean Monsieur Pompidou or any other figure on the political scene; I mean taking care of a proper institutional succession, that is to say restoring to the political institutions of France the power they should have and the role they should play.

So the first question I would address to Professor Kindleberger —which I will state in a counterfactual manner—is whether Professor Kindleberger believes that if de Gaulle had not come to power in France, if the normal parliamentary procedures had been preserved, and that if those curious elements of dictatorial power (mild, I agree, as it is) had not been introduced into the French body politic, would the vicissitudes of the Common Market have been exactly the same as they were in the last few years?

You see, Professor Kindleberger said the Common Market is essentially a political arrangement and not an economic arrangement. Let me try to see by historical reference to what extent this is a significant statement. There was once before in the history of Europe a French attempt to achieve European integration, and that was the Napoleonic Continental System. Perhaps the comparison should not be misunderstood. There are lots of people going around calling de Gaulle a Napoleonic figure, and I'm sure he himself thinks in these terms. Well a man who has never won a battle perhaps should not try to compete with Napoleon, who, incidentally, in addition to winning all those battles, also had tremendous administrative genius and introduced reforms in France which indeed changed the administrative structure of the country. But the Continental System was a truly political arrangement, based on the idea of French supremacy, and it did not survive Napoleon's rule by a single day. Indeed, it inflicted a great deal of permanent damage on a number of countries in Europe, first and foremost on France herself, so that the economic troubles of France in the years following 1815 can be clearly interpreted as survivals and results of the Continental System. This is patently not the situation now. If de Gaulle disappears, the Common Market will certainly survive, and presumably will be stronger than it is now (as Signor La Malfa pointed out).

And there is another problem, which is my second extended question to Professor Kindleberger. As you look at the Continental System, one of its basic deficiencies was an attempt to industrialize, to carry out economic development, without the aid of the most advanced country in Europe, that is to say, England. The situation is not like that now. I think Professor Kindleberger was quite right in mentioning the activities of the American firms in Europe. Europe does not try to carry out its economic development in economic isolation from the United States, and the Kennedy Round is only one example of this point. I wonder—and this is the second question I would like to address to Professor Kindleberger—whether it isn't true that American firms operating in Europe have derived very great benefits precisely from the fact that a high degree of unification has already been achieved in Europe, making possible the paradoxical result that American firms, with their know-how, particularly with their marketing efficiency, have been able to derive the greatest advantages from European unity?

PROF. KINDLEBERGER: Yes.

Perhaps I could expand that statement. I think it's perfectly clear when you compare de Gaulle with the Fourth Republic that he made a tremendous contribution to Europe and to France. But I'd like to suggest that from the standpoint of history de Gaulle will turn out to have been wrong in most of his policies— not with respect to giving France stable government and correcting the deficiencies of the Fourth Republic, but when it comes to, say, being a big-time monetary operator in the world, his monetary policy, he will seem clearly a failure. His withdrawal from NATO after Czechoslovakia—clearly a failure. His insistence on an independent nuclear deterrent, separate policy in computers, separate policy in space—clearly failures. But de Gaulle's basic failure I suspect, looking back later on, will prove to be his belief in the nation-state. The nation-state is finished. It's unwilling to lie down and go away and it will take some time for this to happen, but this is the fact of the matter. I find the greatest insight into this point in some remarks of Servan-Schreiber (in a footnote of page 113 of the American edition to be scholarly about it). Servan-Schreiber says that Sweden has the highest income in Europe. If you look at the Herman Kahn studies of the year 2000, Sweden will be the only country in Europe which is going to have a national income on the level with the Dominions and the United States. But Sweden, he says, is not an interesting example because they're not interested in power; all Swedes know how to do is to live peacefully and make very high incomes. What's wrong with that? I cannot see that this example which is excoriated by Schreiber, I might add by de Gaulle too, proves the French point. What the Swedes do is to find something they know how to do well, and do it. And they do it in a world context. The Swedes have 700 corporations which are international. They have great productivity, a very high standard of living. (We won't go into their suicide rate or their alcoholism—that's something for another occasion.) But I simply want to say that in an economic sense, the Swedes must be doing something right, because they're really not a highly nationalistic country.

PROF. GERSCHENKRON: I warned you not to use the term nation-state and I'm sorry that you haven't paid attention.

Dr. Thorp was asked what the impact on Eastern Europe would be if the E.E.C. could overcome its present problems and whether it would provide enough of an economic attraction to aid in the unification of Germany.

DR. THORP: With respect to the unification of Germany, I think we've gotten into the habit of regarding this as one of the fundamental objectives of life. It's time we puzzled a little over whether or not this really is something which we wish to see brought about or which can be brought about. In the first place, one has to realize that the two halves of Germany have operated separately for such a long time, with such a divergence in institutions, that just how unification would work is a highly uncertain question. But I think the basic question is whether or not the Soviet Union, the rest of Europe, or the United States would like to see Germany united. We all declare this as policy, but as one gets into the question of whether or not Germany then would be a tremendously powerful and strong country, perhaps a threat again to the rest of the world, then doubts arise.

This is all very speculative, but I do have a feeling that substantial pressure towards the uniting of Germany is something one cannot look forward to in the future with certainty. There was an interesting debate which I happened to hear last week among four experts, in which two said that youth in Germany today was bent on unification, and two said that this had rather tended to disappear from their main objectives. Suddenly one realizes that it really is impossible to summarize a state of mind of any group. But I would hesitate very much to make this a problem which is particularly related to the unification in Europe, one way or the other. It's quite possible that to the extent that Western Germany gets satisfaction in playing an important part in Western Europe, pressures and demands for German unification may actually be reduced.

Sig. La Malfa was asked for his views on the role General de Gaulle plays on the European scene.

SIG. LA MALFA: I feel that the constitutional reforms put forward by General de Gaulle are not going to solve the political problems of the French people. The fact that France is ruled by General de Gaulle makes the country look like a country which hasn't got a full-fledged democracy, which is a sort of limited democracy. If France wants to play a European role, it will have to revise substantially its policy when de Gaulle disappears from the political life of the country. And this will call for considerable change and revision on the part of the French political parties.

Prof. Kindleberger was questioned about his point that the Common Market is more a political phenomenon than an economic one. It was asked how politically united the members were, and whether it followed from his analysis that a dissolution of the Market would have negligible economic consequences?

PROF. KINDLEBERGER: What I'm really saying is that the major problems of the world in economics are broader than the Common Market. They are problems of trade, money, capital markets, and corporations, and each one of these involves the Six of Europe. Some of these problems also involve the less developed countries, and all involve North America and Japan. But the major forum for the solution of these major economic problems is wider than the Six, and the Common Market can therefore be a mechanism only for reaching political decisions so that Europe could make a unified contribution to the solution of the major problems. The Dutch, Luxembourg and Italy have been willing to do this, the Germans have up to now, the French have been least willing. As the Germans get stronger and the French get a little weaker, these last two roles may change. But what I'm really trying to say is that the problems that the Common Market is seized with now, in the small, are on the whole less important and less interesting and less significant for economic well-being than the broader problems which demand a solution outside, and where the Common Market with political unity could make a substantial contribution.

81

Dr. Thorp was asked what role COMECON played in the Kennedy Round, whether the Common Market didn't originally want the U.S. to adopt an across-the-board cut of fifty percent, and finally whether he would comment on the role of agriculture in the Community and in international trade.

DR. THORP: The Eastern European countries are not able to play any part in the Kennedy Round. There is American legislation which prohibits any tariff cuts with respect to Communist countries. As a matter of fact, any trade that is done now with Czechoslovakia or with the Soviet Union, is done on the basis of the old Smoot-Hawley Tariff Act of 1930, the highest tariff act that we ever had, and all reductions in the tariffs have not related to those countries. So they're not—they can't be under our present legislation—involved in any negotiations with respect to reducing trade barriers in which the United States is involved.

Regarding the original aims of the Community, they wanted us to make the maximum tariff cut which we could legally make, which was 50 per cent across-the-board. They knew if we didn't cut tariffs across-the-board, but on a selective basis, the most that anybody would get would be 50 per cent and a number of the others would get less. So the across-the-board represented an idea on their part of the United States being able to make the maximum concession. And actually the across-the-board idea did become quite an important one and it was used in large blocks of the tariff area.

Finally, the agriculture problem in Europe is not to get farmers to produce more. There are quite a few agricultural surpluses, particularly in the dairy products field. The new Market agricultural program is in two parts. The first is to give support to the farmer so that he's reasonably well off, much like our own program in agriculture. Since each country had its own scheme, this has required very difficult negotiations. The second part involves what they call structural reforms. These haven't taken final shape yet, but they do involve buying off farmers in various ways, inducing them to produce less, or to consolidate their land hold-ings, or to use better equipment and thus lower costs, and so forth. So the direction that's being taken by the Market is, first, to make the farmer somewhat better off by means of subsidies, and, second, over time to make them better off by some improvement in the structure of industry. I'm not sure that this will cause any great social upheaval—the occupational redistribution of people we're talking about isn't great enough. Europe hasn't yet reached the point where there really is a lot of surplus labor around, and therefore they're at the appropriate point for mechanization, I would say. The social problems in Europe are the normal social problems of most countries where people are dissatisfied with life as they find it, with income as they get it, and I would think that to the extent to which more competition, more research, various things of this sort, either lower costs or improve the efficiency of production, this may tend to somewhat reduce the social pressures that exist in these countries. No doubt about it, in France there's terrific economic dissatisfaction among the people, the farmers, the workers—they feel somehow that they're not sharing in pros-perity, they've got the same sort of state of mind that exists in most of the less developed countries involving demand for higher levels of living. Social upheaval is likely to come if things don't move ahead, rather than as a result of Market action that's being taken.

PROF. GERSCHENKRON: May I perhaps add an observation on agri-culture: if we dare look just a little bit farther into the future and scan the areas where we can expect a considerable rate of growth and considerable contributions to gross national product in the next quarter of a century, then clearly the importance of food-stuffs, the share of agricultural produce in the total is bound to decrease. Even if nothing happens to agriculture and small, inefficient farms are not all eliminated, the importance of agricul-ture and the importance of subsidies paid to agriculture will pro-gressively diminish. It made some sense to write the history of the nineteenth century in terms of the struggle for cheap bread, but now bread, once really the stuff of life, has come to play a really quite unimportant part in overall household budgets. This trend will continue for the rest of agriculture.

Sig. La Malfa was asked whether Italy would give up political sovereignty if the others of the Six did the same, whether he felt General de Gaulle was the only obstacle to a European Federation, and what his attitude was to recent Anglo-Italian initiatives for a new European enterprise outside of the Common Market and provisionally without France.

SIG. LA MALFA: Regarding the first point, my answer is "Yes," because all of the democratic parties are in favor of a supranational power. In fact, if you look at the Coal and Steel Community Treaty, which was the very first treaty made, it referred to supernational power.

As to the second point, I must say I have rather recent experience in this field. I attended a meeting of the Monnet Committee for the United States of Europe, which was held in London on the 10th of March, and on that occasion there were British delegates as well as French delegates (of course not Gaullist ones), and we agreed in the final statement of the meeting on the need for establishing a federal power.

Thirdly, the initiative you mention was taken by the Italian government and the Labor government in Britain within the Western European Union. Some political steps were taken, with a very negative reaction on the part of France. The French refused to take part in this meeting of the Union. The Italian and the British governments now seem to agree in carrying on this action, being mostly concerned with NATO problems, with East-West questions, and the Middle East question.

Professor Kindleberger was asked what the purely economic effects of British entry into the Community would be, and which sectors of which economies would be most affected.

The European Economy: Prospects for Unity?

PROF. KINDLEBERGER: I think it's useful to keep in mind some of the economic forces that lie inside countries as they bear on the question of whether to have a Common Market or not. Let me just turn away from the Common Market to Japan for a moment. The Japanese have been resisting opening up their country to imports and foreign corporations very strongly because of the fact that they have a lot of weak small firms. But now Japan is starting to turn to more openness because of the fact that its large businesses can succeed so well on the outside. I think this is exactly what's happened in Europe, and it's exactly what happened in Britain. In the case of France, the French learned in the Schumann plan that the larger French steel companies, for example, could hold their own with Germany. And at that point, large business in France, which had been protecting small business, decided possibly they'd do better to play on a wider scene, and they prepared to open up their imports. This would hurt little business—rationalize little business is the way they put it, make it more effective, induce it to organize more efficiently—and big business could then extend its reach outside. Now I think this is on the whole inevitable, but it has some painful consequences for small firms, just as the 35 per cent increase in the minimum wage of last June had painful consequences for small French firms. The small firm everywhere is in trouble.

With respect to Britain, the chemical, automobile, and computer people came to think they could handle themselves in competition with the Common Market, in fact do fairly well, so this is the group that decided to go ahead with it. It's little business, the small shops of the Midlands and Birmingham and so on, who resist. This is the competitive effect, as we say in economics. In other words, to many people the Common Market makes a real contribution not in simple old-fashioned comparative advantage terms, but in the competition it gives to what previously were secluded and sheltered firms by wiping them out. This is not very friendly to the companies themselves, but it has a salutary effect in the longer run. I remember a British foreign office man saying

85

it is not true that every kick in the tail helps, some just hurt. But the British have agreed to join the Common Market in part because some of the big firms think that a kick in the tail would be very salutary for small business. I think it's the chemical industry, ICI in particular, the computers, ICT and its successor, which is way ahead of the competition in Europe, atomic energy, Rolls Royce engines, automobiles, these are the companies that are prepared to sacrifice their little friends.

A question regarding the economic and political implications of rising Italian Communist strength in the rural areas was directed to Sig. La Malfa.

SIG. LA MALFA: It's very hard to tell you in a few words about the position of the Communist party in Italy at present. Their success is mainly due to the difficulties which arose from a very long period of depression which we went through in our country, and we hope that it will decrease in the future along with economic advances. The Communist party today in Italy is going through a very deep crisis, an ideological and political crisis, caused by recent international and domestic events, which probably means their impact will decrease.

Prof. Gerschenkron was asked how the Soviet Union fit economically into Europe.

PROF. GERSCHENKRON: All I can do is to explain why I don't think I can answer that question. Like everything else in the Soviet Union, the problem is essentially a political rather than an economic one. If ever there was a primacy of the political factor in history, it certainly has ascertained itself in the history of the Soviet Union. Right now the Soviet Union still finds itself in the prolonged throes of the succession crisis that started with the death of Stalin, and it is altogether uncertain what the future will bring. I think it's an entirely open situation. Russia may still revert back to Stalinist policies. It may march through a number of crises, perhaps with the help of the military, to a much more open situation, or it can go on lingering in that curious grey twilight between the Stalinist night and the dawn of a much brighter and happier future. And as far as Russia's position vis-à-vis the European community is concerned, for the moment, for clear political reasons, it has been all negative. Books and articles have been written full of abuse and exaggerations about the Common Market. The European Community is described as being an additional tool for the exploitation of the toiling masses, still another instrument in the service of monopolies. The atmosphere certainly is not favorable at the moment, and for the immediate future I don't foresee any change in this respect.

3

European Society: A New Generation

MR. VAN LOON: By way of introduction I would like to observe that in each of the previous sessions the greatest amount of disagreement among the panelists seems to have come over the question of Charles de Gaulle. So, although the general does not qualify as a member of the new generation, perhaps it might be appropriate to begin this session with a quotation from him that epitomizes differences in generational outlooks. General de Gaulle once wrote, in complete seriousness, not sarcasm:

> How sad and tragic it is that old age is so disastrous, that faults are so magnified by years. Why could he not relinquish office at the right time? Ambition had taken hold of the empty shell of past glory. He is now an old man dominated by egotism. He loves power. He's flattered because they came to pull him out of retirement and put him back in the saddle. It's only human. But his attitude is not as disinterested as he claims. It's the attitude of an old man who wants to take hold of the reins. That is why he is dishonoring himself in this adventure.

Needless to say, President de Gaulle didn't say that last year. He said it a number of years before—29 years to be exact—when he was a mere lad of 50, before he had come to power. But the contrast between his words and his thoughts then, when he was speaking and writing of Pétain, and the way he felt last May when students were quoting this back at him, suggests that the passage of time and changes of perspective are some of the sources of generational differences.

During the past year these differences in outlook and values manifested themselves widely. Throughout Europe from Berlin to London and from Rome to Warsaw, the streets have been alive with the sound of students. In the May days in France, General de Gaulle was shaken, the National Assembly was dissolved, and a new one formed. But these kinds of events did not occur only in France. A couple of months earlier, in March, ten thousand students marched and rioted against the regime in Warsaw. Students played an active part in creating and helping to further the events in Czechoslovakia. And in Belgium last year, disagreements over Louvain University, and the languages to be taught and spoken, brought down the Belgian government, and caused new elections. In the same year Berlin was forced to change mayors, in large part because of student disturbances and the student-initiated disagreement with the regime. So not only does the new generation look at things differently. It also acts to insure that the effects of its views are felt.

In order to provide a context for our discussion, I would like to mention three things about the New Generation of Europeans. The first is that we hope to examine here not only students but the non-student population. In contrast to the situation here in the United States, students are a relative minority of young people in Europe. In our country, forty-three percent of all those of college age (age 20–24) are enrolled in colleges and universities, but in the Soviet Union, for example, the figure is 24%; in France it's only 16%; in Germany 8%; in Italy 7%; in Britain 4.8%. So we should be careful not to focus on students exclusively.

The second point to be emphasized is that there have been two different foci of student protest and disagreement: the one, of course, is the universities; the other, society as a whole. French students, for example, protested last year that French education hadn't changed since Napoleon and that enrollments had increased

89

substantially faster than facilities. Although the percentages of students seem to us small, we should remember that since 1962, in Britain, in Germany and in France, the absolute number of students has doubled. This of course has put tremendous pressures on the universities.

And students have protested in areas that span both universities and society as a whole. For example, in Nanterre, a partial cause of the French student revolt was as simple a thing as social regulations. Students protested that boys were never allowed in girls' rooms in dormitories. And as one of the French students told me last summer, "Of course this business of being a revolutionary is a full-time job: you can't be a revolutionary just from 10 to 10. You have to work on all aspects of society."

The third thing I'd like to emphasize, is what I perceive to be a new spirit, a fresh spirit, particularly among European young people, in contrast to the more formal cultured image that many of us in America have of the adult generations, or of Europe as a whole. One of the most widely spread wall placards in Paris last year said "Distrust Sad People." Another one read, "Underneath the Cobblestones—There is a Beach." And in England one of the posters put up at the Hornsey College of Art read "Strong Winds Sweep Us Together, Light Airs Carry Our Thoughts." Still another one defined the revolution as "the quiet noise of wisdom working."

We focus first on Germany. Less than a year ago, the British Broadcasting Company brought a group of student radicals to London for a BBC program called "Students in Revolt." During that program, or shortly afterwards, there was a teach-in at the London School of Economics. Gathered on the stage were Daniel Cohn-Bendit and Alain Geismar fresh from the May days in France, Jan Kavan who had been active in the Prague spring, Karl Dietrich Wolff, the head of the German SDS, Luca Mendalese from Italy, and others from as far away as Japan. But in the press and radio reports about that teach-in, the person most widely quoted and most widely identified was none of the individuals I've named. Rather, it was a German student who spoke with perception and reflection, and who said that "Action without reflection tends to become blind and hollow; it can kill the movement." That person was Ekkehart Krippendorff.

Mr. Van Loon then proceeded to introduce Dr. Krippendorff, emphasizing that he is no longer a student, but currently a visiting professor at Queens College, New York. The chairman mentioned that while Dr. Krippendorff was teaching in Berlin in 1965 he had criticized the administration of the Free University, being subsequently relieved of his duties, this action becoming a cause célèbre among German youth. Dr. Krippendorff was also introduced as a co-founder of the Republican Club, a center of the "extra-parliamentary" opposition in Berlin.

DR. KRIPPENDORFF: I'm going to be very brief at this point. As far as I can see, what we are talking about is only partially a generational problem and only partially a student problem, even though generational and student aspects tend to be for various reasons in the forefront of unrest, dissatisfaction, and increasingly articulate political protest movements in Western Europe and in other parts of the world. They tend to be in the forefront, but this is a transitional phenomenon for several reasons. To begin with, I think we should try to understand what presents itself as student unrest, not in terms of what a new generation might feel, for in fact feelings are diffuse and unstructured and are the reactions to given structures, but rather in terms of a reaction to a given society. We should not talk about the new generation, but rather what kind of society do we live in, and what are the reasons that this society has produced such widespread unrest and alienation at this point in its most articulate sectors of the young generation. Thus I think we should turn away from the students, and talk about society, about political structures, and even more about economic structures.

It is much more relevant to phrase the problem this way because we then see that societies and political structures, which superficially appear very different from each other, tend to react very similarly to similar phenomena, be it in Mexico City or Warsaw, West Berlin or California. My own hypothesis is that all systems are developing in such a way that political structures regardless of their economic content tend to become aloof. They are no longer responsive to the people, who are themselves more aware and more conscious and more interested in their own affairs. Political leaders fail to give the people credit for this interest or to let them act on the basis of their own awareness and consciousness, and the true level of their political and social involvement.

The fact that we now have a student problem only points out that the university in a particular way enables this conflict to be articulated and to be brought into the open. It does so because students are students, which means they are young and in a period of their lives where they are relatively uncommitted and non-committal, where they don't have responsibilities towards families, jobs, security, and so on. Consequently they are more free and more able and willing to take certain risks because the risks are relatively low (you may anticipate being sent to jail and being busted by police, but these are still very marginal risks). Also, in certain respects a student has the chance (particularly students in the social sciences who have been in the forefront almost everywhere) to find out more about his society and about its structure than other segments of the population might have. Or to put it differently, the academic community in general, and a student community uncommitted to job security in particular, has more of a chance to gain insight into political, social and economic structures, and possibly can act upon the insights and convictions gained. Thus, and this is my only point right now, students do play a transitional, perhaps a trigger role, as we have seen in France, but they are not a class by themselves. Students today are a group which is not going to be easily integrated, because the society which has produced student unrest is still with us. We cannot expect unrest to disappear as long as certain ills in society are not cured. What these ills are is what we should talk about.

MR. VAN LOON: I mentioned before that there were a large number of wall placards that have expressed many of the views of young people in Europe in the last year. Recently in Britain, a conference occurred at which the theme was "Education Means Reason and not Revolution." The response of French students to this was a different placard, to the effect that people who have nothing to say are probably too busy chewing their cud. But Britain is different. While French students think of an assault on de Gaulle, and German students think of an assault on the West German regime, in many ways young people in Britain, from which our next speaker comes, see something of a British cultural assault on the world. The Beatles, the Rolling Stones, Carnaby Street, King's Road—these have in many ways greatly affected the thinking and feeling and the changing values of young people throughout the Western world. So those who smugly say that the sun has finally set on the British empire just don't realize that the empire has changed to a sort of a cultural sphere of influence.

By way of introduction of our next speaker I might say that there was a period of time in May, June and July of last year when Oxford, Cambridge and the London School of Economics, the schools normally prominent in the papers in Britain, were pushed to the side, and the British educational institution holding the headlines, the mouse that roared, was tiny Hornsey College of Art, located in a northern suburb of London. At Hornsey the students seized the building, refused to let outsiders in, began cooking their own food and running their own infirmary, abolished the old curriculum and created a new one, and wrote a number of tracts. The revolt at Hornsey spread to a number of places: to Croyden, to Birmingham, to the university at Hull, to Sussex. L.S.E. of course was always active. This led even the mighty *Times* of London to observe editorially that the last weeks of the summer term were seeing something of a collapse of order in English universities.

Mr. Van Loon then introduced Kevin Mansell as a former leader in student affairs at Cambridge University.

MR. MANSELL: I've never spoken on behalf of my generation before. Indeed, this is the first time I've been called upon to represent the youth of Britain anywhere, so please forgive any signs of nervousness or, alternatively, paranoia. I have tried to strike a balance. I'd also like to make an apology in advance—to the students of this college—for appearing as a student from Britain clad in a tweed suit. It's a disgrace and I'm ashamed to be explaining what British students think while dressed in a tweed suit. I'd have preferred to have appeared in my customary pea jacket and denim levis but in recent weeks they've begun to disintegrate from constant wear. Please realize how difficult it is for me to preserve student consciousness dressed like this.

I should also say that in Britain, even at very formal academic occasions, students nowadays are little concerned with speakers' sensitivities or social niceties, no matter how auspicious the figure. Clark Kerr gave an important university lecture in Cambridge last year and no attempt was made to spare his feelings in the question period. I think this approach is healthy and honest, and I would welcome it in response to what we have to say.

Our task in this session is to consider how students and young people in our respective countries regard their political and economic systems, to discuss the types of student groups which exist, and to give our views on such matters as whether and how far political parties serve as vehicles of dissent. The title of the discussion, "European Society: A New Generation" demands that we not limit our remarks to student attitudes.

But the necessity of avoiding this last trap provokes some hesitation on my part. I went to a university, as did the majority of my friends. Thus what I have to say about general political attitudes among young people in Britain does not carry anything like the same authority my judgments might on student affairs.

This obligation to differentiate between students and young people in general is especially important in the British context. It doesn't seem to be very widely appreciated in this country, as Eric said, just how unique America is with regard to the proportion of its youth that's getting a college education. In Britain only 8% of the relevant age group goes to a university (I think Eric's figures are a bit out of date). And even that constitutes a proportion which has risen by 50% over the last five years. Slightly over 80% of the relevant age group receives no further full-time education after leaving high school, and 60% of all British school children still leave school at the age of fifteen.

So you see that if we confine our discussion to students, then in the British case we neglect the vast majority of young people. As we shall probably be discussing student protests, I think this is an important qualification to make. I don't deny the importance of what's going on in the universities. After all students are always supposed to be a society's future élite, and the situation of students in being free from career pressures and the consequent need to conform, and mostly unburdened with family responsibilities, gives them a good deal of free time (more in Britain than here, mercifully)—a good deal of free time to reflect, theorize and criticize. But we must face the problem of precisely how particular student attitudes, which may or may not be gaining increasing support in student circles, are to arise or be transmitted to young people who are already out at work. My hunch is that at least in Britain most young people are not significantly more politically concerned than previous generations were. I can conceive of them remaining quite contented with George Bernard Shaw's characterization of a democratic system as a balloon which politicians allow to descend once every five years, allowing some exchange of passengers, and which then ascends to the sky again, with very little continuing contact between the politicians in the sky and the electorate on the ground.

First of all I'd like to deal with what's going on in the British student world. Most of my generalizations will be drawn from my Cambridge experience, though I've read a good deal about events in other universities. Cambridge is still, with Oxford, something of a law unto itself, though to a diminishing extent. It still has a higher than average upperclass intake from the public schools (and public schools in Britain are private schools—you have to pay anything up to a thousand pounds a year to go there), and a lower than average percentage at Cambridge are students from working class backgrounds. Nevertheless Cambridge showed the usual manifestations of student unrest. It achieved national prominence with two very hostile demonstrations against the Prime Minister and Defense Secretary who addressed meetings in the town last year, and this past semester the first sit-in was staged. This had a peculiarly Cambridge flavor, I'm told, in that on reaching the selected building for the sit-in, the Senate house, the demonstrators found it occupied by members of the university Purcell Society who were practicing for a concert. Having elected not to disturb them, the demonstrators moved to an alternative building.

An important point about British students, though, and I don't say this out of sheer perversity or to try and choke this discussion from the start, is that the vast majority of them are pretty complacent and nothing very dramatic is happening in the way of a radicalization of student political attitudes. Most people at University are there for the single-minded purpose of getting a degree, and their political commitment is no greater than that of the average man in the street. Most students spend their time working, playing sports, drinking beer or port according to their tastes, and watching movies, as they do here mostly. Surveys done at three British universities not very long ago, showed that three-quarters of all British students take virtually no part in formal political activities at University. Sad but true. Just how indifferent students are to their immediate environment, to what one would have thought to have been their obvious concerns, I learned from bitter experience on the Student Representative Council, where we met almost unshakable apathy in trying to organize support. I was always amazed that the administration treated us with the respect and the attention that it did. Most students were not even aroused by the action of the government in making an award on student grants last year which will mean a decline in the real standard of living of students in Britain by about twenty percent in the next three years. At Cambridge, 400 people, out of a total undergraduate population of 8,000, took part in the sit-in, and at one stage according to the student newspaper they were joined by 800 people who had to be restrained from evicting them. A petition circulated which in a few hours collected 1500 signatures opposing the occupation.

I know that there's at least one person in this audience with direct experience at the London School of Economics. If I'm not careful he's going to challenge the validity of these assertions. The London School of Economics I would claim to be no more representative than Cambridge of British universities in general, though this term it was closed down for some time. Even at L.S.E., which has been the focus of student militancy in Britain and the center of much of the publicity, the vote of the student union supporting the occupation of the school last term was reversed in a new vote which was necessitated by the presentation of a petition containing 600 signatures opposing the occupation.

I hate to bore you with all these facts, but I think they should put in perspective any notions that may be current about a whole generation of students in ferment, at least in Britain. A noted British political scientist, Bernard Crick, described the prevailing climate of opinion surrounding student unrest as the product of "almost a conspiracy of mutual flattery and exaggeration between a handful of revolutionary socialists and television," and I think that's a fair description of the situation back home.

This is in no way to deny the importance of what the student activists are saying and demanding, but simply to examine the extent of their appeal. The growth of student protest in Britain, and the growing voice of the revolutionary Left, is to my mind

97

closely associated with the experience of what was traditionally supposed to be the socialist party in Britain, now in power. Anthony Sampson, in his book, *The New Europeans*, which Mr. Barraclough mentioned yesterday, and which is quite a good light read on many of the subjects we've been discussing in this symposium, sums up the fortunes of the Labor government rather well. "The British experience seems to show," he writes, "more poignantly than the coalitions in Germany and Italy, how little room for maneuver was left to a left-wing government. As long as the country was in debt, the conditions of international loans dictated economic policy while the weakness of the pound dictated most foreign policy." Slightly later on he claims: "What the British experience seems to show most clearly is that a socialist party can only retain its right to rule if it is prepared to make bold choices based on its beliefs and that the policy of keeping the options open leads inevitably towards loss of prestige abroad and loss of votes at home." There has been a large theoretical debate as to how far the Labor Party has ever really been a socialist party. But for the purposes of the point I'm trying to make, all that is important is that many left-wing students genuinely believe that at an early stage, the possibility of a socialist alternative *was* there.

Parenthetically, since we're supposed to be talking about a new generation, it's interesting to speculate what in fact constitutes this generation, and how many years the generation spans. My own definition of the generation I belong to back home would probably be that its first clear political memory, in the sense of an event which we argued about and in which we felt involved, was the 1962 Cuban missile crisis, which occurred when I was in what you call 9th or 10th grade. In domestic terms our political awakening would probably have occurred in the last year of Conservative government, which left office in 1964. Most of our political views have thus developed in the time of the Labor government.

When I joined the Labor Club in Cambridge in my first term in 1965, the government was still fairly popular, though there were already some criticisms, mainly from hard-line Marxists or Trotskyites. In the period since then, however, the government has forfeited almost all of the student support it had on coming to power, because of a succession of policy measures which I don't want to go through in detail. The most important would be the failure to disassociate from American actions in Vietnam, the succession of economic measures little different from or worse than the measures which the Labor party always used to criticize in opposition, taken to try and improve our chronic balance of payments deficit, the failure to deal effectively with the illegal Rhodesian declaration of independence, and many others which I could specify.

The crowning blow to any faith many of us had left in the government came in a further round of deflationary measures in January of last year, when prescription charges for medicines were reimposed, which the Labor party had always crusaded against in opposition and which it had removed on coming into office, one of the first acts it took in 1964. It imposed charges for school milk (British school children have for a long time been provided with a free third of a pint of milk each day). At the same time, the raising of the school leaving age from fifteen to sixteen, originally scheduled to take place in 1970, was postponed to 1973. All these were relatively minor economies in relation to total government spending, and it appears that they were made solely to impress our foreign creditors.

Students on the left can now in broad terms be divided into those who still see some hope for progress towards a more socialist form of society through the parliamentary success of the Labor party, and those who have abandoned all hope of fundamental change through the existing institutions of parliamentary democracy. Though much student protest is directed towards facets of university life and university teaching, a good deal of it to me appears to be the product of a far more widely related discontent with parliamentary socialism. This has led to the basic tactical decision that if left-wing students are powerless to influence the course of a Labor government's policies (as indeed the party conference has been in the Labor party), then revolution must begin at home by confronting the university authorities—who in the standard militant scheme of analysis are as much an integral part of the repressive social system as any policeman or United States general—to confront the university authorities with a series of demands.

As regards this general increase in militancy and its relation to the national political situation, I would say that developments in Britain bear direct comparison with the change of tactics of German radical students after the formation of the Grand Coalition. Increasing numbers of radical students see little difference between the policies of a Labor government which has failed to live up to its socialist ideals and the Conservative government which it had replaced. I'm not saying I totally subscribe to this view, though my patience is pretty well exhausted, but many students on the left would characterize me as being mystified beyond salvation.

The second source of inspiration behind the radical student attitude is a growing attack on the role of the university within a capitalistic economy and society—its role in supplying the highly trained and specialized manpower demanded by an advanced technologically-based economy. This line of critical analysis has grown remarkably quickly among left-wing students in the last two years. Ekkehart is far better equipped than I am to pursue this point and I'll be happy to leave it for our later discussion. But quite simply, many left-wing students now despise capitalist society and are anxious to destroy any mechanism by which a capitalist economy seeks to impose conformity to its values and to its system of social relations. I'll be more specific if you want me to later.

Someone asked Professor Barraclough whether he thought China posed any threat to Europe. In a farfetched sort of way there almost could be. It's coming in the form of a little red book of thoughts. Many left-wing students in Britain derive considerable inspiration from the forms of economic and social change being attempted in China and Cuba. Sampson says in his book that to leftist students "the whole world of technology, technocracy, political parties, and corporations," and incidentally I think he could have added economic growth, "is becoming completely irrelevant and hostile to their own ambitions and designs." For increasing numbers of politically alert students, this is a fair statement of the position.

I now venture onto far more treacherous grounds and that's the attitudes of young people towards Europe. Much of what I have to say is in general terms from now on, and it will be based on hunch. Indeed, more and more I shall be representing the views of young people on the Left in Britain. Some of the things I have to say may be very tactless, and I realize that there are a number of people here from all over Europe, much of whose life's work and political activity has been devoted towards the pursuit of European integration in its various forms. Consequently, I claim the traditional license of youth—to be immature, inconsistent and impetuous (unlike the two other members of the panel I am only just eligible to buy liquor in the state of Connecticut) and I plead your indulgence. For my own taste, this Symposium has been rather suffocating in the prevalence of sober, moderate, reasoned discussion of various issues. I've never been able to believe that any more than a small minority of people's political beliefs were the product of anything but psychological and emotional factors and I don't dare to include myself in that privileged group.

I'd like to deal briefly and admittedly in a superficial way, as I dare not take much more of your time, with some of the specific things I've heard in the course of the preceding sessions.

I was very interested in Professor Baring's remark that his generation felt strongly the frustration of being a European, and that they considered themselves children of America in some sense. I'd say that many of us now feel quite differently. Some of my American friends have approached with great caution, presumably fearing my embarrassment, the subject of Britain's demise as a world power. In fact it's a non-problem. Who wants to be a superpower these days? Who wants to devote 10 to 12% of the country's national product to defense expenditure? Who wants to have to maintain a nuclear superiority of 4 to 1 over the Russians? Who wants to deploy an antiballistic missile system? Some of us in Britain are sick of the sight of the Labor cabinet ministers' wives launching unwanted and obsolete Polaris submarines in the last few years. My hope for Britain is that she will go beyond the empty rhetoric of us all being "citizens of the world," and actually do something to break the tragic complacency of advanced countries with regard to the enormous economic needs of the under-developed world. Many of us regard the Common Market as primarily designed to help rich people get richer, and thus as a diversion from our real obligations to this wider world.

Secondly, I would say that to a generation born since the war, the intricacies of European security attract little or no discussion or attention. NATO many of us see as part of an interacting system of alliances in Europe reinforcing mutual hostilities. I'm willing to admit we probably don't think enough about the problems of German reunification, or Berlin as the "flashpoint" of the cold war, but there you are. And I don't feel that the Russian invasion of Czechoslovakia has significantly altered this mood. Most of us saw the Soviet action as a cynical and hypocritical maneuver, but I think our reaction was far more one of sickened resignation than of renewed fervor over the importance of NATO. I don't think many of us saw Czechoslovakia as any more than the desperate move of a frightened authoritarian regime, and I would say that our conviction is that that occupation can never suppress, on any more than a short-term basis, the growing emancipation and independence of young people in Eastern Europe from authoritarian communism.

Now just a few more scattered points. The most obviously striking point about our discussions to me has been the over-whelming concern with what appears to me to be the attitudes and opinions of élites. This was epitomized somehow in Professor Barraclough's remark about the Salzburg and Edinburgh festivals being examples of growing cultural convergence. How many people in Britain know when the Edinburgh Festival takes place, let alone attend it? The point I would like to make is that élites may be all very interesting, but just how far are they of lasting significance in the affairs of nations? And if they are, should they be—should we not be more critical of the meaning of this kind of political engineering for ordinary people. I realize all this is very naive and superficial, but it's not yet been mentioned here.

In international relations, I don't think young people (especially students) of my generation see the barriers between Eastern and Western Europe surviving in their present form much longer. To many students in Europe, they're non-existent already. There's something of a similar approach in our opinions of our respective societies, and remarkably common themes are emerging in the way of solutions. One last parting shot on this. Professor Barraclough spoke of a European consciousness as being "a system of values and a way of life." I wonder how many students would agree with him? I wonder what sort of contrast we'd draw between the actions of the Paris police, the Berlin police, and the Chicago police, as evidence of a distinction of a system of values and a way of life in Europe from America.

Finally, I'd like to suggest some topics for discussion. How far does the growth of militant student opposition portend wider dissents in society at large? Where and how is contact with the working class to be established? What sources of conflict remain in the system, or was an American radical right in the SDS conference at Philadelphia over the weekend when he moaned: "The trouble with workers is they just don't realize how oppressed they are." Another rueful German student preferred Lenin's crack that "if German workers ever decided to seize control of a railway station they'd buy their tickets first."

The working class in Britain is at present enormously hostile to student militancy, and it's not easy to see how ideas are supposed

103

to spread from students to the working class. I began by drawing a distinction between students, and young people in general who often in Britain very much resent students. Undoubtedly there's been a revolution in cultural values, Carnaby Street and all this rubbish, life styles, morality and so on in postwar years. But how far is this really significant in political terms? Capitalism can easily absorb changes in fashion, indeed it thrives on them. Similarly with hair styles, though drugs may pose more interesting conflicts.

Personally, I see the dilemma laid out in a very simple way by one of the most widely influential Englishmen of the century (among young people, anyway). I refer of course to John Lennon. Reading Beatles lyrics always sounds a bit absurd, but I can't manage the falsetto bits in the song, "Revolution," and I don't want to attempt to lead mass community singing. So may I quote:

You say you want a revolution
Well you know we all want to change the world
You tell me that it's evolution
Well you know we all want to change the world.
But when you talk about destruction
Don't you know that you can count me out.

Don't you know it's gonna be alright
Alright Alright.

You say you got and real solution
Well you know we'd all love to see the plan
You ask me for a contribution
Well you know we're doing what we can.
But when you want money for people with minds that hate
All I can tell you is brother you have to wait.

Don't you know it's gonna be alright
Alright Alright.

You say you'll change the constitution

Well you know we all want to change your head
You tell me it's the institution
Well you know you better free your mind instead.
But if you go carrying pictures of Chairman Mao
You ain't going to make it with anyone anyhow.

Don't you know it's gonna be alright
Alright Alright.
Alright Alright Alright Alright Alright Alright Alright Alright.*

Very profound sentiments I'm sure you'll all agree—or subtle capitalist manipulation of youth? I think these words may live to haunt student revolutionaries for years. Maybe it's all a question of freeing minds ultimately, in that until people's fears, anxieties, individualism, self-interest and apathy undergo profound change, the new generation in Europe will be little different from the past ones.

Mr. Van Loon then proceeded to introduce the last speaker, Lars Tobisson of Sweden. The chairman remarked that Mr. Tobisson had the double burden of representing the smaller countries of Europe as well as young people. Two other points were also emphasized: that "I Am Curious (Yellow)" had stimulated American interest in Sweden—not only in sex but in the implications of sexual emancipation for young Swedes, and that the high Swedish standard of living, paralleled by high suicide and alcoholism rates, perhaps suggested the future course of development of other countries. The chairman mentioned that Mr. Tobisson was a past President of the National Union of Swedish Students, but also familiar with this country, having studied for a year at the University of Oklahoma.

MR. TOBISSON: Since I am the only representative from one of the smaller countries in Europe, I think I'd better start by giving you some basic facts about my country.

There are not too many of us around. Sweden now has 8 million inhabitants. The population is very homogeneous—there are no ethnic or religious differences. During the last hundred years Sweden has undergone a rapid change from a backward agrarian society to a modern industrial state. In 1870, a hundred years ago, 72% of the population was active in agriculture, and only 10% lived in the cities. Today it is the other way around. The farmers comprise less than 10% of the population. Over 75% of the population lives in cities and towns with more than 500 inhabitants. As Eric told you, modern Sweden is a rather affluent society. The per capita income is $3,600 a year. An industrial worker earns on the average 2 dollars an hour. That means that Sweden has the highest standard of living in Europe, and in the whole world it ranks second only to the United States.

Sweden is a parliamentary democracy. The Social Democratic Party has governed the country since 1933, that is for 36 years. And our present Prime Minister, Mr. Erlander, was elected to that office in 1946, so he has been Prime Minister for 23 years. In the 1968 elections the Social Democrats received 50% of the votes, the three non-socialist opposition parties about 15% each and the Communist Party 3%.

Sweden is a neutral country. We don't belong to any power bloc—neither the North Atlantic Treaty Organization nor the Warsaw Pact. Sweden is not a member of the EEC, but it does belong to the EFTA along with the other Nordic countries and Great Britain.

Out of the total population of 8 million, about 3 million or close to 40% are 25 years of age or less. The main occupation of these young people is, of course, studying. The Swedish educational system has gone through many important changes during the last few years. Ten years ago most youngsters did not get more than seven years of schooling. Now we have a compulsory nine-year comprehensive school, where the pupils remain together in the same class and take the same subjects as they move upwards through the grades. It's pretty much like the American system.

106

And after completing the compulsory education, 85% go on to secondary school for two or three years. Close to 30,000 or 27% of all nineteen-year-olds then go on to college, where it takes three to five years to get a Bachelor's degree. And 27% means that we are rather close to the American figure and well above some of the other countries we are talking about here.

The Swedish educational system has expanded tremendously in the sixties, especially at the higher levels. In 1960 there were 35,000 students enrolled in the universities, today there are over 100,000. This has, of course, led to overcrowded classrooms, a more unfavorable student-teacher ratio, and fewer personal contacts between teachers and students. A big problem is that it has not been possible to increase the admission of students to the most coveted fields of study, such as medicine, dentistry, and engineering, as fast as the total number of students has gone up. Most students, therefore, have had no other alternative but to study the humanities and the social sciences. More than half of the Swedish students are now in these fields. Unfortunately, liberal arts graduates are not in very great demand in the labor market. They already have difficulties in getting employment after graduation. The seriousness of this problem is emphasized by the fact that the annual output of liberal arts graduates will almost treble in the next five years.

One prominent aspect of Swedish life is the strong position of the different interest organizations. Almost every citizen belongs to such an organization from the cradle to the grave, so to speak. I might mention that I am working nowadays for the Central Organization of Swedish Professional Workers. We have about 75% of all college graduates in our organization, which works just like a trade union. Even the salaries of the clergymen are determined by collective bargaining. Anyway, working through organizations is a way of life for the Swedes.

The students, of course, have their own organizations. They even start in elementary and secondary school. At each school there is a local council affiliated to a national organization called

The Swedish High School Students Union. This organization represents practically all of those going to high school and quite a few of those going to elementary school. It aims at greater self-government for its members and has many education reforms on its program.

All undergraduates are required by law to join the student union at their university or college. All of these student unions belong to SFS, the Swedish National Union of Students. The local unions organize a lot of social and cultural activities, of course, but their main function is to represent the students in their dealings with university authorities, and with the municipal administration in the cities where the universities are situated. The SFS has at present 82 member unions with a total membership of about 120,000 students. SFS looks after the interests of its members and deals with the problems relating to education and programs of economic assistance to students. The local unions build and administer student dormitories and restaurants, health services, and so on. SFS is also involved in international student affairs. On the national level, SFS works as a regular interest organization. It has a lot of contact with the authorities, and much of the work consists of drafting and making statements on proposed legislation. SFS is also regularly invited to nominate representatives to various royal commissions looking into fields of interest to students.

In addition to SFS, there are many other student societies. For example, there is a student association for each of the political parties. The professional associations also have their own student groups. I might add that there are some SDS groups in Sweden, but their following is rather insignificant at present.

My own immediate contact with student organizational work dates from the mid-sixties. I was President of the student union at the University of Gothenburg in 1963 and President of SFS in 1964. And in my present occupation I am in a position to follow rather closely what happens in the student world.

I think that the most important change during the last few

years has been that students have become much more interested and involved in political and ideological matters. During my year as President of SFS, there were hardly any dissensions along political lines at all. Our approach was practical and pragmatic, and everybody cooperated regardless of political opinions. Student leaders were elected on the basis of personal merit—not on the basis of affiliation to a particular political party. Now, however, there are parties at almost all the big unions, and they put forward slates of candidates at the elections. These parties usually have some kind of connection with the national political parties.

It was the students of the Left who brought politics into the student unions. After they had had some initial successes the non-socialist students followed suit. And today the students of the Right are in power at all five big university unions.

One result of this change has been that the student organizations have lost some of their former effectiveness. Internal political fights sap a lot of strength and sometimes the unions don't even act as interest organizations any more. Student leaders now demand more power for students in university affairs, but at the same time they tend to look down upon traditional pressure group activities.

One point that you can make about all Swedish students, I think, is that they are very internationally minded, much more so than just a couple of years ago. They are very well informed of the situation in faraway countries. Their attitude might be described as one of global moralism—they are highly critical of the U.S. involvement in Vietnam, of the suppression of black people in South Africa and Rhodesia, and of the policies of the military junta in Greece. They are very much in favor of increased aid to the developing countries. And as I said, this is true of practically all students, even those belonging to the parties of the Right.

Although the non-socialist student groups are in power at all big student unions, their leftist opponents are more active and therefore draw much more attention to themselves. They attack the existing order and criticize the Social Democratic Party for not being radical enough. They like to point out that although the Social Democrats have been in power for almost 40 years, as much as 90% of all Swedish industry is still privately owned. So they maintain Sweden couldn't be called a Socialist country. They call themselves Marxists but often show anarchistic leanings. Herbert Marcuse, Rudi Dutschke, Che Guevara and even Mao Tse-tung are held in high esteem. I might add that last May revolutionary students tried to copy the events in France. They set out to occupy the Opera, for some reason, but didn't succeed. They only succeeded in occupying their own student union building in Stockholm. But there have been several demonstrations where students have not refrained from using violence.

The opinions and activities of the active minority on the left fringe has caused angry reactions from the older generation. There is in Swedish society right now a considerable antipathy— and even hatred—against students in general and student demonstrations in particular. These feelings seem to be most pronounced among the workers and among those who have not had a chance of getting an education for themselves. Here I'm repeating what Kevin told you before—we have the same situation in Sweden. One frequently voiced demand is that students who don't stick to their studies should be stripped of their scholarships and student loans and put to do manual work.

This adverse reaction has incidentally hurt the Communist Party, which lost nearly half of its former number of votes in the fall elections of 1968. This was due partly to the events in Czechoslovakia last summer, of course, but also to the fact that the party was associated with the student demonstrations and the occupation of the union building in Stockholm. The leader of this occupation was on the slate of candidates put forward by the Communists in Stockholm, but the workers, the trade unions, pressed for his removal. They didn't succeed, and many workers turned away from the Communist Party as a result. It appears this development has not run its full course as yet—the Communists are still losing their traditional strongholds in the trade union movement, and workers seem to be fleeing the party to join the Social Democrats.

Thus there is at present in Sweden a clash between different political ideologies and between different generations. The older generation has fought hard to improve its economic situation, and won't tolerate anything that threatens to prevent a continuation along the same lines. The students—or rather a very active minority among them—want to crush the present social and economic setup and build something more compatible with their own ideals. It is too early to predict exactly what will come of this confrontation. I have a feeling that the fact that the revolutionary students have not succeeded in getting any substantial support from other groups in Swedish society will mean that no radical changes will take place. But the student unrest will no doubt leave some marks on the established order.

MR. VAN LOON: We have a wide range of problems that our panelists have thrown out as possible topics of discussion. How far does student militancy reflect wider discontent? Could we focus on the sources of conflict? What about student-worker ties? What avenues are open for social change? What is the future of student movements? Are they dying out as Rudi Dutschke recovers from his wound and Cohn-Bendit remains banned from France? All of these are provocative and complex questions.

Mr. Mansell was then asked whether worker-student cooperation was possible when students were the very élite he mentioned as going to the Edinburgh Festival.

MR. MANSELL: About the Edinburgh Festival, all I said was that I did not want generalizations to be made about growing cultural affinities in Europe from the fact that some people went to the Edinburgh Festival. That's just a cliché being thrown around. I don't believe this is significant for European integration.

With regard to the problem of students being in some sense an élite group, in Britain the middle class *is* still far overrepresented

111

in higher education. Yet compared to some other countries, Britain has a very favorable record. I think our percentage of working class students at institutions of higher education is about 25%, whereas in France, it's perhaps as low as 5%. I'm not sure and stand to be corrected, but I believe in Germany it's very low as well. So in that sense British students are less of an élite group than in other European countries. With educational reforms going on in Britain, one would expect to see a growing working class in the universities. Of course, the real problem is that the working class has always been discriminated against far lower down the educational ladder: through an examination at age 11, through a tripartite system of secondary education, and so forth. The Labor Government is now supporting a system of secondary education which should be far less discriminatory, but it remains to be seen how well this will work.

There are enormous problems in instituting student-worker action. I can give you specific examples in Cambridge, where there are two areas in which students on the far Left have been attempting to establish contacts with workers in the town. In one case, the Cambridge City Council, which is controlled by the Conservatives, hiked the rents on public housing by 10%, and they put forth very dubious reasons for doing it. Students belonging to the Socialist Society of the university cooperated with the local "Rent Action" committee, an ad hoc organization that was formed to fight the rent increase, canvassing public housing estates attempting to make information available to encourage people to stand in opposition to the rent rise. They've been very unsuccessful, and very disappointed. In a local election that took place in one ward recently, a ward affected by the rent increase, a Conservative candidate supporting the increase was returned. Moreover, the percentage of the total electorate voting was 40%, which is not a sign that the working class people in Cambridge are yet ready to respond to student initiatives.

Another case in Cambridge politics that I'm familiar with relates to one of the features of European integration, namely the international take-over movement in business. Cambridge has a very very low concentration of any form of industry, the largest firm being a British telecommunications company which has just been taken over by the Dutch electronics firm, Phillips. Redundancies were created in the process, and Phillips has decided to close down the plant in Cambridge, rationalizing operations and so on. I think about 600 people were thrown out of work, and that's a serious business in a town where there's not much alternative employment and wages are very low anyway. Students have been attempting to organize there as well, but again with little success.

So there are two specific cases of students going out and looking for issues on which they can ally themselves with the people in the town. They're not meeting much success as yet, you're quite right, and there's still a lot of suspicion of these sorts of initiatives on the part of students. There are hardened attitudes in many university towns, because the freedom of the young people at University contrasts with the sort of life that young people at work lead. And facilities are often grossly unbalanced, the sort of entertainment that's available is unequal, and so forth. There's a vast amount of suspicion to be broken down, but I suppose it's only in small ways like this that you ever begin the sort of social revolution that's going to be needed.

A member of the audience then asked Mr. Tobisson if he could explain how Swedish society came to be so highly organized into groups.

MR. TOBISSON: I don't know if I have one clear-cut explanation. One thing you might say is that Swedes seem to have some kind of capacity for or interest in organizational work, and this interest in organizations is not something that is restricted to students, but extends to all groups in society. Organization of students in Sweden started in the 1920's, but SFS did not achieve a prominent position until around 1950. At that time we had as President of SFS the present Minister of Education, Mr. Olof Palme. Another

113

active official in this period was the present head of the Employers Association in Sweden; another of them was my boss, who is now chief of the Central Organization of Swedish Professional Workers. These people, who were active around 1950, have gone on to prominent positions in Swedish life, and that helps their successors to make contact with different seats of power. Also, student leaders are respected among the authorities and the university professors. Indeed, professors often say, "It's much easier for students to get in contact with the authorities than it is for us, so can't we work out an agreement so that you take a proposal that has originated with us to the authorities because then it will have much greater chances of success?" I can't give you a more clear-cut explanation. I don't know the situation too well in other countries, and don't know if this system could be transplanted to United States. But that's the way it works.

Also, Swedish authorities are perhaps more flexible when it comes to university affairs than they are in other European countries. For example, we have had student representation in decision-making bodies at the universities for quite some time. Now there is pressure for more of that kind of representation and the authorities are agreeing. There's no problem. Even the university professors agree; they are a little reluctant, but they know that they probably won't have a chance to stop it.

The panel as a whole was then asked whether the uproar of the last year had really achieved any significant reforms.

MR. VAN LOON: I'll say one thing quickly. Earlier I mentioned the placard in France that said "Beneath the Cobblestones There is a Beach." There are placards up in Paris now that say "Beneath the Cobblestones There is Only Mud."

DR. KRIPPENDORFF: The question we always have, you see, is what kind of demands are you talking about and within which period of time. There is usually in these situations a pattern where some demands are raised, they are refused, and demands then escalate.

The first set of demands is then perhaps met, but by that time, the level of conflict has drastically risen. In all cases that I know of, the original demands were very much limited to immediate grievances within a given university, a given institution. They were often personalized demands, such as asking for the resignation of this or that official. The reaction of university administrations or national governments revealed attitudes in these administrations or governments which brought out facts about the quality and the structure of those institutions that were not originally evident. Consequently, the protests have increased and were altered from attacks on individual officials to attacks on the structures of our institutions and even society as a whole. At that point the question can no longer be compromised. It is relatively easy to replace an official, be he a university president or a President of the United States. It might even be possible to replace de Gaulle. But when demands rise to such a degree, or when insights into the situation, the structure, the economic, social and political conditions have developed to such a degree as to recognize basic structural defects, then to meet these demands would mean in fact a revolutionizing of society. Thus we have today, at least in West Germany, in France and in Italy, a pattern of demands which are now being met on the university level, allowing student participation on a limited or even a relatively wide scale, and where certain individuals in leading positions are being replaced. But that stage is long past; it does not any longer coincide with the level of consciousness of those who originally raised those demands. Consequently, the meeting of these demands becomes objectively and subjectively irrelevant.

MR. MANSELL: It appears the situation in France is that extremism —the Cohn-Bendit leadership, the Geismar leadership—is losing support amongst French students to a Communist-sponsored faction of the National Student Union. You remember, it was the Communist Party that was on the defensive and that most students seem to have abandoned it as a force for change last May.

As far as Britain goes, the situation is quite interesting because we had our round of sit-ins in the spring of last year, with much direct student action, occupation of buildings, and so on. And the effect this had was in favor of the respectable, responsible National Union of Students, which the militants had rejected. The militants put forward a lot of demands, but the Vice-chancellors responded by agreeing to deal with the National Union of Students. The agreement that's been reached is on the demands of the National Union group, namely effective student presence on all relevant college committees; secondly, staff-student control of discipline in internal hearings and appeals; third, staff-student departmental committees to discuss course content and teaching methods; fourth, radical reform where necessary of examinations; and fifth, abolition of all paternalistic outdated rules and regulations, and the creation of staff-student committees to settle internal rules by mutual consent. There's nothing very revolutionary there at all. These are all demands that the National Union of Students has been making for years, and they've been falling on barren ground. Now, because the Vice-chancellors were becoming very frightened at what went on in the spring of last year, they've made rapid progress.

MR. TOBISSON: I might add some remarks concerning the situation in Sweden. The call for university democracy which is heard more often on Swedish campuses right now is a new catchword, but there is an old tradition behind it. Our latest university reform took place in 1964, while I was President of the SFS. The position of the students was considerably strengthened. They had had representatives before on the faculty subcommittees responsible for educational matters, and as President of the local union in Gothenburg in 1963 I sat in on all faculty meetings and had frequent contacts with the President of the University. But in 1964 the number of representatives on these educational subcommittees was increased, so that there were 3 professors, 3 students, and

116

finally one representative of the assistant teacher category, who might be described as half student and half teacher. Each department of the university, such as the Economics Department, the History Department, also established its own decision-making board with 2 student representatives. These boards deal with all questions confronting the department, except the appointments of professors.

We have also started to experiment with even more delegation of power to bodies with equal representation for teachers and students, a demand put forward by the student organizations. This is now on an experimental basis. We're trying to figure out new ways of governing the different departments and faculties at the universities.

There's one more interesting point. The students on the far Left demanded for a while that the running of the university should be turned over completely to the teachers and the students. I believe these demands were inspired in part at least from outside the country. Anyway, they caused a rather sharp reaction from all sides. The Minister of Education, Mr. Palme, pointed out that the universities should not be isolated from society at large. He said that the costs for higher education were paid by tax money from people who had never gone to university themselves. And the least the taxpayers could ask for was to have some control over the way this money was spent. Mr. Palme called for a greater integration of the universities into society as a whole. And one way of achieving this goal, that is being discussed right now, is to create new governing bodies for the universities, whose members would come from outside the academic world. There would be representatives from the trade union movement, from the employers' associations, from the local city government, and so on. Changes along these lines are resisted mostly by students on the far Left, on the one hand, and conservative students and teachers on the other. This peculiar coalition appears in many different contexts. The students on the far Left and those on the far Right

117

unite in their criticism of the middle road politics of the Social Democratic Party, and this is shown in many different aspects of Swedish university life.

MR. VAN LOON: I might add one thing, quoting Daniel Cohn-Bendit, Danny the Red, on precisely this question. On the 20th of May last year, when the strikes were going full blast, when the Sorbonne was still occupied, before de Gaulle had made even his first speech, let alone his second, Cohn-Bendit had a long interview with Jean-Paul Sartre. Sartre asked this same question and Cohn-Bendit, even when it looked like de Gaulle might fall, responded that it was really silly to talk about revolution. That wasn't really in the cards. What we think will happen, Danny said, is that radical revolutionary demands will result primarily in moderate reforms. You won't abolish the bourgeoisie or workers' desires for fundamental economic gains. But out of the radical action will come some moderate social reforms, and then those social reforms will be seen as not enough. Also, we've proved that radical action does get results. And we've proved that you just can't say, it can't happen here. Perhaps at some time in the future a combination of student demands and worker demands will coincide and result in major social changes.

The panel as a whole was then asked how students who are demanding change could take the responsibility for the changes and developments that would follow on their protest.

DR. KRIPPENDORFF: If I interpret you correctly, you would say: "Look, what you want to do is all very nice, but do you realize that this is actually a destructive process? You might wind up with a dictatorship or something worse; these left-wing radical people might produce something which they didn't want at all. Can you take the responsibility?"

If I may be rhetorical, I would return this question, and say, all those people who are now in charge of the politics of our society, can they take responsibility for the things which are going on here every day? If they can take that responsibility, then I can too. I can take the responsibility for the things I propose to do. Anybody who can face the present state of affairs with a good conscience, and can justify—in this country or in West Germany or in France, or in any country involved in big or small power politics—what they are guilty of (I don't want to use moral terms, but what they are responsible for), if they can take that responsibility, then I can too, regarding my responsibility for advocating changes. But that is of course a rhetorical answer.

If I answer your question perhaps more fairly, well, Kevin quoted a Beatles song with one line which is repeated over and over, in which people say look, we're all for you in principle, we are against the Vietnamese war, we are for more student participation, we are for all the good things, but please give us the plan. We want to have that blueprint. I challenge anybody who asks this question and claims to be serious. I think he's not serious. If you ask for a clear-cut plan for the ideal future society, you implicitly already reject any answer you might get, because any plan presented is bound to have so many loopholes, built-in mistakes and failures, that anybody with two semesters training in political science, for example, would be able to demolish it. That is the wrong question to ask.

Now again, rhetorically speaking, when in 1776 Americans started a revolution, it was not a peaceful revolution, let's face it. There was quite a bit of bloodshed. So perhaps they should have argued more with the British administration. If I take today's lines we would have to say the Colonists should have convinced the British slowly and peacefully. But no, they took to arms and it was a violent uprising. To return to the point, those who engaged in the 1776 revolution didn't know exactly what they wanted. They knew in general that they wanted something which they called a democratic Republic. They wanted elected officials. They wanted the people to be responsible somehow, to be in charge of their own affairs. But they could not predict all the consequences and all possible developments. They could not give you that blueprint which you now demand of radical students. Do you then want to accuse the early Americans of irresponsibility for starting a revolution on the basis of the vague general principles of the Declaration of Independence? After all, the Constitution came quite a few years later. What I suggest is that we should look not for blueprints, but rather at that change which is now taking place—a process within which new institutions, new organizations, new forms of communication and social interaction are being practiced. It is not then the question to devise a blueprint for a new university, but to change the situation in the classroom, the relationship to your teacher, by being at least as qualified in your knowledge, or at least in the questions you are able to ask, as your teacher is, by changing thus your relationship between teachers and students in general so that faculties might eventually become sort of senior consultants. This is a process which can at a later point be ratified in terms of a new university charter. But that's not the main point. The main point is this process of a changing of social relationships, in a university and in other situations and other environments, out of which then evolves or develops a new society. Whether this means a change of the Constitution is more or less irrelevant.

MR. MANSELL: When I was active in student government, we were in a sort of cross fire between silence on the part of the majority of the passive students and very very heavy criticism from a small minority of people on the extreme Left. We were always vilified for the fact that our demands were too moderate, that we were prepared to cooperate with the university authorities too much. Most of us felt that there was never really any case for change unless there was some broad base of democratic support within the university. University administrators are not fools; they know when you're speaking just for yourself and when you're speaking for an important feeling on the part of the large majority of the students. I think a problem that faces people who do hold fairly radical views about the way society should be reorganized is that

120

you will always need to convince, to persuade, perhaps to educate, to suggest possibilities to the vast majority of people. I don't think change can be brought about by a minority. In that way there will be violence, and perhaps a sort of worse repression and a backlash from the authorities sooner or later.

That's why I was a moderate back home, quite apart from the fact that I couldn't often stand the rhetoric and the intolerance of people on the extreme Left. I just don't see that change ever comes about without some broad consensus. Even if it's a minority that's actually working for change, there's got to be a broad sympathy with the aims. I would have thought that was true of any revolution.

The discussion then returned to the question of élites, a member of the audience arguing that an emphasis on the necessity of educating the majority of the people was too conservative, that one would thereby "wait till the cows come home." It was stated that the insight of the radical minority (defined as an élite) was most important.

MR. MANSELL: Marcuse says there's no point in having worker control until we get a completely different type of worker, because otherwise it'll just be used for solid material gains. What's the point of worker control if it's as bad as control by someone else?

DR. KRIPPENDORFF: This emphasis on élites puzzles me. It gets the discussion going in the wrong direction. In one respect, of course, it's correct to say that you have no right to demand or agitate for or to put into action revolutionary changes if you don't have something like a qualified majority behind you. Otherwise you wind up with what we've got in the Soviet Union. On the other hand, your point is equally correct. If we wait for that, we will never get anywhere.

The answer, I think, is shown in the practice and practical experiences of the last couple of years in Western Europe (as well as in this country). That is to secure a majority base within clearly defined environments like a university or even a given factory. We had, after all, an example in France of certain factories being taken over by the workers (who were then abandoned or betrayed by their union officials, by the Communist Party). Also, today in West Germany there is practically—and I simplify now—no university where the politically active students do not constitute a majority, and where the Left does not occupy all the leadership positions. Consequently you *can* press demands and *can* feel justified in pressing demands because you have the needed majority. The same is true for Italy: it's hardly reported in the American press, but there's practically no Italian university which has functioned properly in the last year; the majority have been closed down for months. These developments can serve as examples for other areas of society.

What we should not look for is 51 percent of the electorate. That is not the issue. But 55 or 70 percent of a given area, of a given profession, a given institution, a given factory, or a given laboratory—that's what's called liberation here—to liberate certain areas of the productive sectors, and thus in the long run bring about social change much more effectively than by asking for the general political majority. We have to go back to the grassroots of the productive process (and the university is, after all, a productive factor of enormous importance). We have to go back to the productive process, and if a majority is secured there we then can go further. That's why this so-called new politics tries to avoid the trappings of the old politics in terms of playing the game of organized mass politics, of organizing a new party, of getting elected, of playing the game within the system. That's what we need to change because the rules of the system are precisely established or laid out in order to curb qualitative social change.

MR. MANSELL: I still don't understand how you make the transition from these sorts of strategic victories to a parliamentary victory. You can seize any number of factories you like, but until you've got a socialist plan in operation, nothing very different is going to happen to society. Just when does the normal system of parliamentary elections and of government come into your picture? How does the transition take place? How are working-class attitudes changed?

DR. KRIPPENDORFF: Well, parliamentarism is a very complicated subject and I don't want to go into it. But I think it is fair to say that parliaments can and should be forced to react to changes in the social structure. They should respond. The old-fashioned concept of parliamentarism involved nothing but ratification of social compromises reached somewhere else. Now if you return to this scheme then you can ask Parliament to please ratify this or that change, to make a law of it. You can say, if you don't we will have changed it anyway, and Parliament will become superfluous. In West Berlin we had this sort of situation within one Institute, the Political Science Institute of the Free University. Here there was a change in operations brought about by student-faculty cooperation. This new order, and a new charter, had to be formally ratified by Parliament. Normally, Parliament drafts a new charter, then they listen to every party concerned—to the students (well, before, they wouldn't have to listen to the students), to what the professors have to say, what the university administration has to say, and so forth. The new process was exactly the opposite. The students and faculty at this Institute adopted a new charter and said, this is our new charter. Parliament, take it or leave it. If you don't ratify it, we are going to practice it anyway. So Parliament was forced to ratify this charter and make it law.

The panel was then asked if there were any distinctions to be made between student movements in Eastern and Western Europe.

DR. KRIPPENDORFF: It's very difficult to say because all of us have very little knowledge, really, of what's going on. We know something about Czechoslovakia, but who knows about Poland? Who knows about the Soviet Union? I know very little about East Germany. Who knows about Bulgaria or Rumania? This is really a question of knowledge, of information.

MR. VAN LOON: Last year I spoke with students from the Soviet Union, Poland, Bulgaria, Rumania and Czechoslovakia, but I still have difficulty, certainly, in answering the question. In one sense, the goals of Eastern and Western student movements seem to be different. The difference is the one that Stephen Spender mentioned in his recent article in the *New York Times Magazine*, namely that a great deal of emphasis in Eastern Europe is put on gaining basic human freedoms—freedom of the press, freedom of speech, freedom of expression—that we in the West are supposed to have achieved. Czechoslovakia would appear to be a case in point. But I think that this is misleading—and many Eastern Europeans hasten to reject this description. They feel very uncomfortable when the Western press characterizes events in Czechoslovakia, for example, as a movement towards Western values and away from a Socialist system. They find that as insulting, silly, and inaccurate as the recurring allegations that every American activist or civil rights worker must be a Communist.

In Eastern Europe they feel that they have achieved a basic state of socialism—in terms of factors of production and ownership. They've never lived under capitalism and have no desire to move in that direction. But they do have an idea of a more perfect form of socialism, what the Czechs call socialism with a human face. This image, this ideal of socialism is what they have been taught in school in the same way that we learn about what democracy is or should be. Then, just as our notions of what democracy should be were jolted when we saw Chicago last summer, the realities of their life clash with what they see. So their movement for social change is a move towards what they feel is a higher form of socialism, a more perfect kind than what exists, and this involves bringing in the human face, the basic freedoms.

A more real point of difference is what many Eastern Europeans perceive to be the limitations of the social visions of some Western radicals. They emphasize that a socialist economic system alone is not enough; that socialized medicine alone is not enough; that neither insuring widespread education for everyone, nor getting rid of poverty are themselves sufficient to create a society in which each individual grows to his fullest potential. Some Western radicals, and particularly German SDS members, share this perspective—that it's one thing (an easy thing) to say that we in the West have freedom of speech and a free press, for example, and let's applaud the Speaker's Corner at Hyde Park. But don't be misled by the emptiness of that. In Germany in particular, the emphasis is on not just being free to say what you want (and not being put in jail if you say it), but rather on having the ability to have one's views spread widely to reach people. For in Germany, the Springer press has a virtual monopoly on much of the press, and those on the Left are less able to disseminate their views.

DR. KRIPPENDORFF: In the press and elsewhere there is an emphasis on the differences between the West European and American and the East European movements. And of course, if you look for differences you'll find empirical evidence for them. You can, for example, report conversations going on between the West Germans and the Czechs, in the spring of 1968, where there was a lot of misunderstanding.

But if you look more closely, and are more closely familiar with these discussions, you will find out that these disagreements are disagreements within a large area of agreement and mutual understanding; that actually all these student groups or New Left groups in Western and Eastern Europe have more in common with each other than with their individual national establishments. And the same holds true if you widen that to America.

I think one should stress that for whatever might come out of it, we now have something like a European solidarity on the Left fringes in each country. That's not relevant, perhaps. But what is undoubtedly relevant, is that in the most articulate sectors of politically active groups, there is a new trans-European solidarity, which defines itself not only negatively in terms of their individual establishments but also positively in terms of a socialist transformation of society. That holds true for West European, for American, and for East European movements. None of them restricts its goals to just free speech movements. These were the beginnings—in Czechoslovakia, in Berkeley, in West Berlin, in Tokyo or wherever. But in all areas, particularly Eastern Europe and the Atlantic area, we now see a development towards a socialist ideology, of course on a different level and in a different structural environment and context in Eastern Europe than in the West. But it's certainly there in both cases. Those in East Germany, for example, who protested against Czechoslovakia (and for the first time there were something like a hundred arrests in East Germany, which is still almost the most peaceful state in the world in which to live); and the slogans of these people were "The Invasion of Czechoslovakia is Detrimental to Socialism." This was not an attack on "Soviet imperialism" and all that, but rather to say that this is a blow to socialism. And the people in Poland are definitely socialists. We don't hear much about Poland at this point, but the manifestos which have been produced are socialist. Similarly, in West Germany and France, in Italy and in the United States, you see this development if you watch carefully. The positive goal is some sort of socialism. Exactly how this will look—don't ask for the blueprint!

The question was then raised whether the seeds of unity that seem to exist among student movements might produce a European, an Atlantic, or even a world unity in a generation or two.

MR. MANSELL: I'd like to think so but I have my doubts, simply because of the small number of students with radically different notions of society in their various countries. The obligation lies on them to try and widen their movement, to enlarge their following, to build contacts with the working classes, as I've said, and

I think the transformation must come about within individual countries first. It's true as Ekkehart says that there is a comradely band of students throughout Europe, who may meet quite regularly and may appear on television programs in England, and this enforces solidarity, keeps their spirits up and so on, but until the basic problems of enlarging their support within their own countries is solved, I don't see anything happening.

DR. KRIPPENDORFF: I have a feeling again that the direction of the question is wrong, even though that's usually the question that's being asked. I would say the question should be: who cares about unity or not unity—political unity of Western Europe or of the western world? Let's assume we have a European President, a European Parliament; would that make the world any better or more peaceful? The content counts, not the political form. Unity is not a goal in itself, but it's the content of that unity. I foresee that we are not moving towards unity, but towards a sort of dispersed authority, of decentralized powers. If radical movements are able in the long run to destroy their national establishments (and it is the national establishments themselves which create power politics and investment in armaments and all that), we might develop a new type of community on the basis of dissimilarity. You can't forget that the British are different, that they have different traditions than the West Germans or the East Germans or the Italians or the French. These should not be wiped out and everyone put into one melting pot. But it's primarily a question of the content, the economic, political and the ideological structure of these societies which makes them peaceful or not. Unity is not the prime goal. The unity of Europe, if it comes about, is fine if it's socialist, but if it's not, then not.

MR. TOBISSON: Most Swedish students are not very fascinated by the idea of European unity. I don't think that this concept is very much in their minds. Indeed, when you talk to students now they often ask: why should we have something in common with Europeans in particular? Why shouldn't we feel a solidarity with all citizens of the world or with students in the developing countries? Many feel that if the European countries banded together, particularly in the economic field, that might be a threat to the developing countries. The students feel we shouldn't erect any barriers to these countries and to closer contacts with them. This is one strain of thought, and there are of course others, but I think it is rather significant that most Swedish students (and I think students in the other Nordic countries too) are not very fascinated by the idea of a European political unity.

MR. MANSELL: If I had to explain briefly what I think is the attitude of British youth to Europe, I would point to Harold Wilson's case for entering Europe. He's more or less abandoned the straight economic argument, and now emphasizes the need to establish a European technology so that we're not dominated by American technology. The prize example of this argument, the forerunner of this trend, is the Anglo-French Concorde, the supersonic airliner built by an Anglo-French corporation. We're ahead of the Americans here it's argued; this is the wave of the future. But many students are deeply critical of the Concorde business, for it's a prize example of the way European technology could go. Here you have an airplane costing Britain up to 300 million pounds I think it is now—it'll probably be more before we're through. And what's it designed to do? It's designed to carry— I don't know how many—over a hundred businessmen at a time over the Atlantic in 3 hours instead of 7 hours. When you consider the opportunity cost of that investment in terms of what could be done within British society now on improving slum primary schools or slum housing or—well, Prof. Barraclough argued that Europeans were very Americanized now in their consumption habits. I'd loved to have pointed out then that a third of the dwellings in London have no bath. Government reports suggest that there are still vast areas of backwardness in our economy, people living in decayed houses, and so on. One of the things I would support that the Labor government has done in the last year is to pull out of the European space launcher, the E.L.D.O. project. Why on earth Europe should get involved in a wasteless deployment of resources in trying to get men to the moon, I simply do not know. I just don't understand how people make these judgments when there's so much more directly of benefit to people in our societies that could be done. I don't even think the balance of payments arguments are very impressive.

PROF. CALOGERO (from the audience): If I have understood you correctly, you have often commented on the advantages of socialism. Now many of us in Italy, including Mr. La Malfa and myself, think that there is really no longer a philosophy of socialism as opposed to a philosophy of liberalism. We feel modern society is going to become both more socialist and more liberal. Societies, even in Eastern Europe, are driven to recognize basic freedoms, but also greater social equality. This is true even of the United States, which is thus a socialist state in some senses of the word. For example, if garbage workers have to be paid as much as university professors, you perhaps are even going beyond socialism to communism. And I approve of these developments. How would you comment on this suggestion?

MR. VAN LOON: It's an interesting question: whether the real issue isn't social equality, and whether one shouldn't, for example, consider seriously whether garbagemen should be paid as much as professors because they're performing—I don't want to say equally distasteful tasks—but if the social value of their tasks isn't the same.

MR. MANSELL: What are the figures for the distribution of wealth in Italy? I don't know offhand the figures for the distribution of wealth or of income in the United States, but in Britain the figures always quoted are that one percent of the population owns 50% of the wealth, 5% owns 80% of the wealth, 70% of the population gets 40% of the income, and so we've obviously got a long way to go towards socialism. At last the Labor Party is beginning, 10

129

years or 20 years too late, to realize that there's something fundamental involved here. Also, I still think power arises out of property, and as long as we have a managerial class that decides whether people should be made redundant, as long as these decisions are the privilege of a small group of men with privileged higher education, then I don't think society's changing at all. I don't think socialism means equality of income, it's just a different system of men living with men.

A Postscript

by Jan Kavan, Head, Section for Foreign
Relations, Union of University Students
of Bohemia and Moravia (S.V.S.)

July 3, 1969

Thank you for sending me a transcript of your Symposium Session on "European Society: A New Generation." I should also like to thank you for the opportunity of joining your discussion, at least in writing, as American authorities made it impossible for me to visit you and discuss the subject on the spot. Incidentally, I must admit, I am unable to account for this decision on the part of the State Department. Could the stability of your society really be threatened by one Czechoslovak student?

While reading your discussion I was struck by the marked difference between the contribution of Dr. Ekkehart Krippendorff and that of Kevin Mansell. The former remarks, in my opinion correctly, that we should talk about society, about political and economical structures, rather than confining ourselves to students. The latter only touches on these subjects. This can be explained, I think, by the fact that the British student movement, if it can be called a movement, is not expressly a political movement. If I am to speak about the Czechoslovak student movement, I shall be able to link these spheres, because our movement from its very beginning has been a distinctly political one. I shall deal mainly with the Czech student movement, that is to say the movement in Bohemia and Moravia, because the student movement in Slovakia has developed along somewhat different lines, with specific features which are a result of different conditions. I shall give only a brief outline of the history of the movement as I do not like repeating myself: I wrote an article for *Ramparts* magazine last August, and I also spoke about this subject at the N.S.A. Congress in Manhattan, Kansas.

I would place the beginnings of what we afterwards called a movement somewhere in 1963, when student groups began to form within the monolithic, bureaucratic and centralized youth organization, the CSM. These groups demanded a reform of this organization so that students might win a certain amount of autonomy. The students wanted to achieve this autonomy through a federalized CSM divided into age and social groups. This would have provided a platform from which the students could express their political views, which the CSM had not provided. In other words they wanted nothing more than the right to have their own elected representatives, who would be responsible to the membership, that is to the students—who could be recalled by the students and would unwaveringly express and support student views, even if in so doing they should get into conflict with the powers-that-be.

At the National Students Conference held in December, 1965, this demand was formulated by Jiří Müller, spokesman for the radical students, who stressed that the students had the same aim as the Communist Party—the building of a socialist society—but that they wanted to have the right to express an opinion on the ways and methods selected by the Party to accomplish this aim. In 1965 this was a revolutionary demand; the radicals had already won considerable support among the politically committed Prague students. This support grew during the "campaign for Jiří Müller," who was expelled from the CSM in December, 1966; he was immediately sent down from his University and called up for his National Service. During this campaign, the radicals combined the fight against the unjust expulsion of Jiří Müller with a fight for the ideas associated with his name. Within six months the radicals had strengthened their position in Prague to the extent that many of them were sent as delegates to the Fifth Congress of the CSM, which was held in June, 1967, where the radicals hoped to get their reforms accepted. They did not succeed and they could not possibly have succeeded. The CSM leaders, who saw attempts at reforms as an attack on their own interests—their power and authority—"prepared" the Congress very thoroughly. However, the radicals did at least manage for the first time in 20 years to disturb the customary unanimity and sow the seeds of new ideas in the minds of some of the delegates.

A few weeks later another student was sent down from his faculty and called up. The embittered Prague students gave expression to open resistance and began to completely negate the existing structure. They tried to seek contact with other social groups, mainly among the workers, but without much success. Novotný's ruling bureaucracy virtually prevented any horizontal contacts because it rightly saw in contacts of this kind the greatest danger to its own power.

The student movement outside Prague disassociated itself from the radicals and put forward its own more moderate reform program with considerable emphasis on an improvement of the students' standing and conditions. In October, 1967, the now famous Strahov demonstration took place. It was not in itself a political protest: the students were really only protesting against continual breakdowns in the power supply—they wanted light in order to study. The regime under which we were living at that time, however, regarded a public expression of dissatisfaction with social shortcomings as a highly political act. The radicals drew upon their past experiences and in the period following Strahov they managed to unite the student body as an entity, critical not only of conditions at the Strahov halls of residence, but of the regime which tolerated these conditions, a regime which instead of arranging for repairs sent the police against the demonstrating students. The behavior of the police was by Czechoslovak standards rather brutal. In the autumn of 1967 the students thus contributed to the creation of a united anti-Novotný front composed of various social groups.

At the same time they spontaneously founded student parliaments at most of the faculties and resigned from the CSM. As far as the students were concerned, the CSM had been moribund long before they created their own independent organization in May, 1968—the Union of University Students of Bohemia and Moravia (S.V.S.). As I have said, up to this moment students had been bound together by their attempts to rebel against the status quo rather than anything else. Now when they were called upon to put forward a constructive policy, cracks in their unity began to appear, as a consequence of the different levels of political experience and, primarily, of theoretical knowledge. Up till then, students had reacted to given situations rather than creating something new. Their actions had been based entirely on empirical experience. For example, they had seen that in democratic centralism as practiced there was a distinct imbalance between democracy implemented once every few years at elections and centralism operating in the form of directives at all times. They saw, therefore, that democratic centralism in practice constituted a method of preserving power. For this reason they entirely ignored this principle in their own Union: the Union leadership did not have the right to issue directives to the faculties; the presidium's decisions served only as recommendations to the faculties. I could give many examples, but will mention only one. The students hesitated over the question whether the new Union should immediately join the State and Party bodies by becoming a member of the National Front, as their Slovak colleagues had done. They simply shelved this issue and, without committing themselves, leaned towards cooperation with the National Front.

During the spring and summer of 1968 the students fully supported attempts at forming a system which has become known as "Socialism with a human face." They achieved their first successes in forming contacts with workers whom they began to visit on a large scale just after January, 1968, when Novotný and his accomplices tried to persuade the workers that all the post-January reforms were nothing more nor less than a disguised attempt by the new bourgeoisie to deprive the workers of the rights for which they had fought in February, 1948. For some time after January the workers hesitated, and supported the progressive elements in the Party only passively, awaiting the turn of events. However, the workers sharply rejected Novotný's demagogy in January and the students can justly claim that they played a certain, if modest, role in the outcome. Contacts between workers and students were maintained after that, but spasmodically and on a small scale.

I should like to dwell at some length on the activities of students and the young generation in general during the spring and summer of 1968 because these—like many other developments in Czechoslovakia—have been the subject of various false interpretations. Being the first generation to grow up under a distorted form of socialism, we tended towards skepticism. When we were at the primary school, we read poems to "Father Stalin"; by the time we had reached high school, he was being violently denounced. Faced with such contradictions, we found it difficult to have confidence in any leader in whose election we had played no part whatsoever. Therefore, from the outset we did not have unreserved confidence even in Mr. Dubcek. We were not comparing our society with capitalism; we were comparing the theory which we were being taught with the practice that we observed around us. Thus, our criticism of our society was an attempt on our part to narrow the gap between the idea of socialism and the actual conditions we were living in. The events of last year should be regarded in this light. Eric, who probably is the most well-informed of the panel about what was going on in Czechoslovakia, says that a great deal of emphasis is put on gaining basic human freedoms: freedom of the press, freedom of speech and freedom of expression. That is true; I would just add a few more freedoms, like freedom of assembly, freedom of association, in fact all the freedoms expressed in the Universal Declaration of Human Rights, approved by the United Nations in 1948.

Here I should like to point out that we have already had our revolution. Our bloodless revolution of February, 1948, which brought the Communist Party into power, provided an alternative to the pre-war system that had permitted the Munich disaster. Then a socialist transformation of society was launched: private ownership of the means of production was abolished and the power of the capitalists over political life was ended. But the revolution did not pass through all its phases; above all, it did not renew all the civil freedoms of which it had had temporarily to deprive the population. And it did not ensure that the power which the workers had won would not in time pass into the hands of a bureaucratic elite "in the name of the working class." In 1968 we tried to bring the revolution through this final phase and among other things to restore human rights and civil freedoms. I do not mean to say that by doing so we would have immediately begun to live in an ideal type of society which would have needed no improvement. Such a society does not exist and cannot exist. A form of society which does not develop must necessarily, sooner or later, stagnate and play a conservative role. But we should create the basic conditions for the further improvement of a socialist society with the full support and cooperation of the majority of the population. And because Dubcek's reforms created such conditions and enabled young people to think freely and to make free use of the fruits of their thinking, my generation wholeheartedly supported the progressive trend in the Party. Nevertheless, some student leaders stressed that our support did not preclude the possibility that in the future the young generation might formulate its own program which would not necessarily be identical with the program of the progressive part of the older generation. Our support grew commensurately with the Party's endeavor to define more precisely what it meant by the concept of democratic socialism. In April we became acquainted with the Communist Party's Action Program and supported it unreservedly.

These freedoms have a different significance in the context of our society than they have in a capitalist society. There, after acquiring these formal freedoms, it is necessary to pose the question: "Where do we go from here?" The answer is clear: it is necessary to change the whole basis of the system, to abolish the exploitation of man by man, as well as the manipulation of man by man. In this sense we have already gone a lot farther than you, and although there still remains a great deal for us to do, unlike our colleagues in the West, we can identify ourselves with the society which we are criticizing. When students in Eastern and Western Europe are sharply critical towards their Establishment, West European students speak about the necessity for breaking up and destroying the existing structure of society, that is to say they are in total opposition to their regime, whereas we speak about a participatory confrontation.

It is probably when we speak about civil freedoms in the West that our words are most often misunderstood. I'll give you an example. Last year *Ramparts* magazine published my article, "The Testimony of a Prague Radical," in which I wrote: ". . . All rights and freedoms are necessarily related to the economy. Therefore we consider democracy in the economy to be vital. That means for the working people to play a really active part in the administration of the enterprise. . . . For us, the classic civil liberties assume the utmost importance. In a socialist society, freedom of speech, freedom of the press, freedom of assembly and freedom of association are essential if the people are to exercise any control at all. I have often been told by my friends in Western Europe that we are only fighting for bourgeois-democratic freedoms. But somehow I cannot seem to distinguish between capitalist freedoms and socialist freedoms. What I recognize are basic human freedoms." Stephen Spender later extracted this paragraph from its context and quoted it in his book, *The Year of Young Rebels*, adding his own commentary: "Russian intellectuals who are struggling against their government in order to have greater freedom have expressed themselves in very much the same language. The idea that there is a fundamental difference between the kind of freedom that intellectuals wish for in the Communist countries and have in the West is exaggerated. It is the same freedom." This statement is only a step from the claim that we are fighting for what you already had a long time ago. And this claim is being misused by people in the East and the West against us and against the radical Western students.

I think if Stephen Spender had gone on to quote my following paragraph, this kind of misunderstanding could have been avoided. The paragraph in question read: "The point is that in bourgeois society the 'bourgeois freedoms' are in practice useless, for they cannot be translated into effective social action. In a socialist society these freedoms can be the foundation for direct democracy. The working class can play its political role only when it has freedom of speech and information, and freedom to organize. Only then can workers' control of industry be possible."

It is quite clear that in a capitalist society freedom to shout one's head off in Hyde Park does not change anything; it is freedom for freedom's sake and has, for example, nothing to do with workers' control. Until the means of production are nationalized in your society, all liberties are an illusion, of which fact radical students are becoming aware. Those who ignore this fact in connection with these freedoms often maintain the same erroneous attitude when speaking about our endeavors. At this point we cease to understand each other, which is a pity, for I believe, despite everything, that many of our aims and aspirations are the same; only our experiences are different, for our methods, tactics and terminology were created under entirely different conditions. I am, however, convinced that the dialogue which we managed to establish last year with West European radical students, particularly in Germany, France and also in England will continue to benefit both sides. I am convinced that such a dialogue—joint seminars and so on—could constitute one of the measures towards creating a more united European anti-imperialist, anti-bureaucratic student movement.

I read with great interest the remarks of my English, Swedish and German colleagues on the relationship between their student movements and their workers. I think that in this respect the Czechoslovak student movement could serve as an example for many of our Western colleagues. In spite of the fact that for many years Novotný's ruling clique maintained an artificial conflict between the workers and the intelligentsia, we have achieved today a unity such as Marxists only dreamed of formerly. We have no problem in establishing contact with the workers nor in arriving at a common course of action and basic ideas and ideals. Therefore the American radical, quoted by Kevin, who moaned at the SDS conference that "the trouble with the workers is they just don't realize how oppressed they are," probably brings a smile to the lips of Prague students, even if it reminds some of them of the situation in our country five or six years ago. We have found that the workers are capable of very rational thinking; their positions as fathers and husbands and their thorough knowledge of everyday problems often prevents them from sinking into empty radicalism, extremism and anarchy, but it also prevents them from being carried away for long by a full plate, illusions or phrases, whether they are uttered by those in power or by students. It is incorrect to ponder how to "spread ideas from the students to the working class." This formulation suggests that students are convinced that they have a patent on correct ideas. They then only have to spread them to the factories and success is ensured. This contains the danger that the workers will sense that the students feel themselves to be an elite body, and they are very sensitive to this. If students speak the language of their philosophical seminars with a vague idea that it is their duty to kindle a spark in the factories, this, in my view, is very little. For instance, the course of the May events in Paris showed how tremendously important it is to grasp which problems are vital both for students and workers. Students can be successful only if their demands are formulated in such a way that they are putting into words what the workers already feel.

After rather ad hoc contacts with workers during the Czechoslovak spring, we established permanent contacts during our

November sit-in strike. Workers participated in the work of the Action Committee; factories sent us strike funds which amounted to tens of thousands of crowns; cooperative farms sent eight thousand eggs; bakers sent bread, and so on. GPO telephonists connected long distance calls for us immediately, wishing us the best of luck. Our ten-point declaration was endorsed by factory after factory. It expressed what the majority of the population felt; and people knew that "our students" were fighting not for their own interests but for the common cause. It was important that none of the points dealt with specifically student problems:

1) The basis of our policy is and shall be the Action Program of the Communist Party as accepted at the April Central Committee session.
2) There shall be no policy-making behind closed doors; in particular, the flow of information between citizens and their leadership shall be restored.
3) Introducing censorship in the mass media of communication is temporary, and shall not last longer than six months.
4) Freedom of assembly and association shall not be violated.
5) Freedom of scientific research, literary and cultural expression shall be guaranteed.
6) Personal and legal security of citizens shall be guaranteed.
7) Those people who have lost the confidence of the nation and who have never clarified their positions shall no longer remain in their posts.
8) The forming of Councils of Employees (our name for Workers' Councils) as bodies of self-government shall continue.
9) Freedom to travel abroad shall be guaranteed.
10) In the sphere of foreign policy, Czechoslovakia shall not participate in actions which would contradict the feelings of the Czechoslovak people, the United Nations' Charter and the Universal Declaration of Human Rights.

The workers declared support for us, even threatening to go on strike if any attempt was made to silence us. Our "Letter to

Comrades, Workers and Peasants," in which we explained what we wanted and how we were conducting our sit-ins, was telexed from factory to factory.

Secondary school pupils joined us in many places. Open discussions were held between us, young students and workers, both in factories and in the occupied faculties. Factories went on token strikes for fifteen to thirty minutes and blew their sirens.

The strike also helped to consolidate the student movement itself. Both strong factions—the moderate and the radicals—worked together. The strike took place in all (!) faculties throughout the Czech Lands. Students also learned how to coordinate their actions and make use of their specific knowledge. The Faculty of Journalism immediately set up a Press Center. The Medical Faculties had a first-aid squad in every occupied building and a well-equipped First Aid Post. The Film Academy of Arts made a complete cine-documentation of what was going on. One of the technical faculties systematically "eavesdropped" on the police radios and so on. . . .

Immediately after the strike the Government requested from the Ministry of Education a report and evaluation of the strike. In this report, which was very comprehensive, the Ministry of Education, in comparison with governments of other states showed great understanding for the students' efforts and aims: ". . . In the years 1962–65 demands in the student movement were predominantly for students and concerned directly their own or university problems. Gradually, as students began to realize that these demands could not be fully met within the framework of the universities, their critical attitude began to sharpen towards society and the Communist Party, as its leading force. The focus of their demands began gradually to acquire a political character. Before January, 1968, students in their well-meant demands encountered growing resistance from the existing political system. After the Strahov events head-on clashes were narrowly averted. The majority of the students supported socialism ideologically, which was a consequence both of our historical experiences

(Munich, the Nazi occupation, liberation by the Red Army) and of criticism of the manifestations of imperialism in the postwar period (Vietnam, revanchism, the situation in the developing countries, etc.). Our students regarded themselves as an important part of all our progressive social forces and sought in them their allies in promoting social progress. This can be regarded as a positive feature of our student movement in comparison with some adventurist, anarchistic and radicalistic elements of the student movements in the Western countries. . . . In launching their strike, besides the ten points, the students were following some general aims . . . : They expressed their resolution to prevent a return to the pre-January methods in our political life; to establish contact with other strata of the population, particularly the working class, to inform them of their opinions and gain their moral support, to prove to themselves and to the other strata of the population that they are capable of acting in an organized, decisive but disciplined way even under very difficult conditions. . . ."

In the resolution which the Government passed on December 19, 1968, regarding this report of the Ministry of Education on the students' strike, the Government *inter alia* expressed "its deep conviction that even if a misunderstanding had arisen, caused by insufficient information about the aims of the Government, primarily regarding the contents and possible time limit within which it could realize this program, a strike should not have been used as a means of expressing the students' apprehension about the realization of the basic principles of our post-January policy. . . ."

Our alliance with the workers did not end with the strike; on the contrary. In December, the Czech Students' Union concluded agreements with individual trade unions, which were approved at individual trade union congresses. The most well-known is the agreement with the Union of Metal Workers, which, having been the first, became a sort of model for the agreements that followed. Allow me to quote at least part of the section of the agreement which states our common interests:

141

". . . Both parties appreciate highly the fundamental successes of the people of Czechoslovakia in the post-January period, particularly:

1) Open participation by the public, led by the working class, in the creation of State policy and the policy of the Communist Party.

2) The open dialogue between the public and the State and Party leadership conducted by the mass media.

3) The renewal of the social role of the Communist Party, expressed particularly in the Party's Action Program of April, 1968, the reply formulated by the Presidium of the C.P.'s Central Committee to the letter composed by the five Communist Parties in Warsaw in July, 1968, and the 14th Extraordinary Congress of the C.P. of the CSSR in August, 1968.

4) The Czechoslovak people's resistance to the intervention by foreign troops from the 21st to 28th August, 1968.

The Czech Metal Workers' Trade Union expresses support for the recent student strike for the implementation of the ten points put forward by the Union of Students. . . . The Union of University Students of Bohemia and Moravia supports efforts by the metal workers to remove dogmatic functionaries and bureaucrats from the leading organs of the Revolutionary Trade Union Movement and the creation of an organization which would represent the geninue interests of the workers.

Both parties reject the present policy of making continual concessions under external pressure and the intentional interruption of the flow of information between the State and Party leadership and the public.

Both parties protest against the accumulation of functions, power and information in the hands of a narrow group of leading representatives.

Both sides disagree with the fact that policy in the Czech Lands is formulated by an undemocratically appointed C.P. Bureau for

Work in the Czech Lands and demand the immediate convening of a Communist Party Congress.

Both parties reject critical attack on the "cultural front" and appreciate highly the political engagement of cultural workers.

Both parties issue a warning against restricting freedom of expression of the mass media.

Both parties are indignant at the continual postponement of the reappraisal of the new conception of economic development and the postponement of a public discussion and the passing of a law on socialist enterprises.

Both parties demand that facilities be provided for a team of representatives of workers from enterprises and of Czechoslovak economists to work out an alternative economic program. . . ."

Further parts of the agreement set out concrete forms of cooperation, exchange of information and so on. All the agreements concluded in December and January with workers' trade unions are still valid and are being observed.

Cooperation between students and workers has been excellent, for example the joint campaign in favor of Smirkovsky and the organization of various actions (manifesting processions through Prague, the funeral and so on) after Jan Palach's suicide.

Of course, I have to admit that at that time and later the radical students carried out some actions and gave addresses that had a negative effect, owing to the fact that they were not always capable of judging the situation realistically. Despite all these mistakes, one very positive feature stands out, which is that for the first time in the life of this generation of students a Leftish stream was created which had worked up to support of Marxism from the bottom; until then we had accepted the ideals of Marxism only formally. On this level we can confront the Western Left. We must endeavor to modify some practices of socialism; they must mold their thinking not only in the light of ideas but also in the light of our experience.

My remarks have taken up more space than I originally intended, therefore I shall confine myself to brief comments on some problems which were raised frequently in your discussion. It is a pity that I cannot talk to you and reply to your questions, of which, I imagine, there would be no dearth. Perhaps I shall have an opportunity some other time.

Some of the panelists mentioned the question of parliamentary democracy. It has become a habit to draw a demarcation line between the attempt to accomplish social change by making systematic use of the existing structures, particularly the political parties and parliament, and the attempt to create an informal movement of various social strata, to constitute various pressure groups or, as our West German colleagues call them, extra-parliamentary opposition. Both methods have their advantages and disadvantages, of which I am sure you are fully aware. I believe, however, that the advantages of both can be achieved by a suitable combination of both methods, for in my opinion one does not preclude the other. In our student movement, for instance, there are people who firmly believe in parliamentary democracy and we have our student Deputy to Parliament, both in the Czech National Council (even in the Presidium of the C.N.C.) and in the Federal Assembly. They submit students' opinions and defend their interests. The group of radical students inclining towards informal structures and distrusting parliamentary State institutions (because their experiences to date, which they tend to generalize, have not been the happiest) do not oppose the former; on the contrary, they often make use of them, even if at the same time they find other ways of ventilating their views. Both methods can be effectively combined for specific actions and campaigns. This combination and cooperation at the same time prevents each stream from succumbing to extremes and teaches both of them political thinking, mutual tolerance and respect.

The continuity of the student movement from the first groping steps to today's organized state has won for the student body a good reputation with the public, and their campaigns and declarations today have considerable social significance which cannot

144

be overlooked. One of the results of this situation is the fact that since last autumn student representatives have been in contact with the highest representatives of the Party and Government. Meetings, which turn into a lively exchange of views and do not always end in complete agreement, are by no means infrequent. I am convinced that these mutual elucidations of standpoints, confrontations of views, exchanges of information, and so on, are to the benefit of both parties, for they create the basic condition so that neither side can jump to the rash, biassed conclusions which have caused immeasurable damage in the history of our Republic many times.

I should like to conclude these rather incoherent remarks (in which I have tried, on the one hand, to acquaint you with some concrete facts of our movement, and on the other hand to react to the problems which arose in your discussion) with a brief statement about the present complicated situation in the Czechoslovak student movement. The Union of University Students of Bohemia and Moravia (S.V.S.), with a membership of 60,000 students, was dissolved by a decree of the Ministry of the Interior a few days ago. The new, so-called preparatory committee of the S.V.S., which has the full support of the Ministry of the Interior, has not managed to gain the backing of the extraordinary students' parliament which was convened last week. As I am writing these lines the presidium of the dissolved S.V.S. is lodging an appeal against the Ministry of the Interior's decision, and intends to take the matter to court.

The situation is very complex, and the future, as far as the concrete form of a union is concerned, is difficult to foresee. Therefore I shall confine myself to a few facts. The Ministry of the Interior dissolved the S.V.S. under Law No. 126/1968 concerning some temporary measures for safeguarding public law and order. Justifying its action, the Ministry states: "The Ministry of the Interior came to this decision after ascertaining that the activity of the students' union was directed against important interests of the foreign policy of the Czechoslovak State. The Ministry finds proof of this in articles published by leading functionaries of the Union, in the content of various resolutions, public appearances and other actions organized by the Union." The Ministry goes on to state that it could not overlook the fact that the Union's activities had gone beyond its organizational statutes, particularly as regards its public activity furthering political aims and demands, and that activity of this nature could be carried out by the Students' Union (under Law No. 128/1968) only if it were a member of the National Front.

I must explain the connection between the National Front and the Students' Union. The students' congress which met in Olomouc at the end of April discussed a proposal to join the National Front. This proposal did not gain the necessary two-thirds majority. The vote was: 71 for, 70 against, 27 abstentions. Both sides had a number of objective and subjective reasons for their vote. The conclusion was drawn that the decision was fully in conformity with the law, for the Union believed that its interpretation of Law No. 128/1968 was correct in that the Union's joining the National Front was not obligatory under that law. The Students' Union is primarily an organization expressing the interests of the students as a social group; it was constituted in this way and it also works as such. It is not a political party or a political organization fulfilling the function of a party, which must be a member of the N.F. After the Congress, the chairman of the Students' Union sent a letter to Mr. Erban, chairman of the N.F., in which he stressed that ". . . in order that the Students' Union could take an active and responsible part in the work of the N.F. it would be necessary to change its organization so that it would be capable on the one hand of fulfilling the duties arising from the statute of the N.F., on the other hand of operating politically and with some effect and purpose in the structures of the N.F. according to the views of the organization's members. The Congress showed this state of affairs unequivocally. Parliament and the Presidium of the Students' Union therefore hope that this approach will meet with understanding on the part of the leading organs of the National Front." This shows that not even the radicals, who voted against joining the N.F. and were elected to the new Presidium of the Union, rejected the idea of joining the N.F. in the future, after altering the structure of the Students' Union and solving internal problems.

The letter of June 20th, in which the Students' Union was dissolved, however, quotes Law No. 126/1968 as the main reason for dissolving the Union. Therefore I must briefly express an opinion on this reason. As head of the section for foreign relations of the Students' Union, I declare that I am convinced that the Union's foreign policy has not conflicted with the interests of our socialist State. In our documents concerning our international policy we have always described our endeavors to secure peace and social justice. We have condemned American aggression in Vietnam in the strongest terms, just as we have condemned all attempts by world imperialism to suppress other peoples' rights, to solve ideological or territorial differences by military means, and attempts by any country to usurp the position of an international gendarme and to force other countries into national, social or existential disaster. We have supported the struggle against colonialism and neo-colonialism, against all forms of imperialism, occupation and suppression, against dictatorship, and power politics, and the struggle for the dissolution of international military pacts for revolutionary changes and for socialism, in which, we believe, lies the future of mankind. We have condemned the fascist governments of Spain, Portugal and Greece, we have asked for recognition of the GDR, condemned the racial policy of South Africa, expressed solidarity with the people's struggle in Angola, etc.

We have always stated very clearly that our natural allies are the students of the socialist countries and Leftish revolutionary student unions in Western Europe. But, of course, we should like to have bilateral contacts with every student union in the world, except fascist ones, provided they are based on mutual tolerance and respect for different political standpoints. As far as our articles

147

and statements in the Western press are concerned, it is difficult to defend the Union, because I do not know which articles the Government has in mind. But I, myself, have had bad experiences with the Western press. Not only have journalists sometimes misunderstood my statements, as in the case of Stephen Spender already mentioned, but I have also had experience of deliberate distortions. For example, the article of mine in *Ramparts* to which I have already referred, was partially reprinted by a London magazine called *Student* and was completely changed. They omitted all the passages where I was critical of the capitalist system as such, but what is more, where mere omission did not suffice to change the content, they added their own paragraphs, the import of which was the diametrical opposite of what I had written. They did not mention that the article was reprinted from *Ramparts* (although I had specified this as a condition of publication) and later they even published an announcement that I was under arrest in Prague because I had written an anti-Soviet article for their magazine. Also it is impossible to control Western reporters when they quote extracts from our speeches and add their own comments to them, thus sometimes completely changing their meaning.

The Student Union's appeal will possibly be dismissed and the Union will cease to exist. This is a sad fact, because although I am sure we have committed many mistakes (who would not have made mistakes in the complicated situation in which our country finds itself!), I regard the basic aims of the Union of University Students of Bohemia and Moravia as correct and I believe that the future will prove me to be right. It is not possible to dissolve a movement as such; its further continuity cannot be prevented by any administrative means and measures. As has already happened in the history of the movement, the use of such means would lead only to a further radicalization of the students, to a further sharpening of their political awareness. The degree of political awareness among Czech students and young workers is very high today, and this justifies my hope that the young generation will continue to play its progressive role, to support the progressive wing in the Communist Party, and foster the principles of democratic socialism even under the present difficult conditions. As such it can be a worthy partner to those social forces in capitalist societies, who are fighting for the socialist transformation of society, for the abolition of the power of the monopolies and the monopoly of power, for the complete nationalization of the means of production, and so on. I believe that through the united efforts of the progressive youth of the world we shall succeed one day in creating what we should like to call a "happy society," a society in which the biggest problems to be solved will be only the most intimate and personal problems of the individual members of such a society. Let us work and fight together for the realization of this dream.

4

European Politics:
The Relations Between East and West

MR. ZAUSMER: All of us who ever struggled with Julius Caesar and his Gallic Wars know that Gaul was divided in three parts. General de Gaulle sometimes maintains that all of Europe is divided into three parts: Western Europe, Central Europe, and Eastern Europe. I'm glad that those who planned our program did not follow the Gaullist formula, but rather decided on two parts, Western Europe and Eastern Europe. You can argue all kinds of theories: you can divide Europe into North and Central or North and South. But a more natural division, and this is not just a result of the so-called Iron Curtain (which today has quite a few holes and is a bit rustry, but still there), is this division of East and West.

Where is East and where is West in Europe? Prince Metternich once remarked that the Balkans begin at the Land Strasse, one of the districts of Vienna which at that time was on the city's eastern outskirts. As a rule I do not agree with Mr. Metternich, but here he had a good point, because about 60 miles or 70 miles east is the Hungarian border, today's Iron Curtain line. And there is a difference between the areas of Europe west of that line and those east. We can overdramatize and overstate this difference. Previous panelists weren't quite sure what Europe was. We are quite sure there are two parts of it. But if we look at the two halves of Europe, we may also understand a little better the whole of it.

There is no real sharp division; lines are blurred. The various nations or nationalities on either side of the line dividing East and West are not homogeneous. But if you look at this line you will see to the west primarily nations that could originally be called Germanic tribes—the Germans, the Austrians, even the French, the Franks. To the east you have (also in a much oversimplified way), the Slavs—the Czechs, the Poles, the Russians, the Serban Slavs (whom we call the Yugoslavs).

Of course there are others to consider. History works in a way like a glacier. You had a glacier coming in from the east, the Turks, and they moved all the way to the gates of Vienna. They occupied, for centuries, a number of these countries. We sometimes forget that the Greeks, the Rumanians, and others haven't been independent of Turkey for very long. And then there was the Russian glacier from the east. Now, if you go to New Hampshire or Vermont and you see down on the hillside a huge, huge boulder—well no farmer carried that 25 foot boulder there. Rather when the glacial ice disappeared the boulder was sitting there. The same is true for nations, for communities, for societies. When the glaciers from east and west receded, there were groups left, say of Slavs, of Turks here and there, of Hungarians. As the glaciers of conquest moved west and east they deposited some of these boulders. But the primary division remains.

Another related point to be considered is the impact of centuries of Turkish occupation on the eastern part of Europe. It is hard to understand Eastern Europe without knowing of the impact of these occupations and conquests. Western Europeans have a habit of looking down on Eastern Europeans in a very arrogant and completely unjustified way. But if we want to understand why there haven't been democracies the same way as there have been in the West, we have to look back over history and see what the glacier of occupation has done, how it has shaped the boulders, some of them long and narrow, some of them big and round. How it has modified the entire system, the life and the psychology of the people. This matter I would suggest we keep in mind, along with the more obvious problems of East-West relations as we see them today, Communist or non-Communist, and so forth.

Mr. Zausmer then turned to the speakers, remarking that both had a practical knowledge of both East and West Europe. Dr. Svitak was introduced as a scholar and teacher at the Charles University, Prague, now working at Columbia University, and as one who could speak authoritatively about the gallant Czech cause. Prof. Hassner was introduced as Eastern European by birth, now a resident of France, and as a noted expert on international relations.

DR. SVITAK: In 1968, two small nations in Central Europe asked their neighbors, asked Europe and the whole world the following questions: Is it the purpose of socialism to achieve larger human freedom? Can a repressive totalitarian system be gradually transformed and democratized? Are basic human rights, national independence and the sovereignty of peoples, compatible with socialism? Or to put it theoretically, is the original authentic program of Marxist socialism compatible with the reality of the present Soviet state? Are the humanistic ideas of authentic socialism compatible with the interest of power elites in socialist countries? Or to simplify, is it at all possible to build socialism without a Soviet occupation? You know the answer of the Soviet tanks. What are the consequences?

The attack on Czechoslovakia by the Warsaw Pact will have far-reaching consequences for world policy, for the Soviet bloc and for Europe. The invasion itself was carried out in only a few hours, but the consequences of the Soviet adventure will emerge later—at the moment when statesmen and nations realize the shocking parallel with Munich, 1938. A leading European statesman was then convinced that by his appeasement of the aggressor, he, Chamberlain, had saved peace for one generation. But you know he only postponed war by one year.

The most serious result of the Soviet occupation of Czechoslovakia is the change in the European scene. Leading politicians are nowadays seeking a continuity of the policy of bridge-building, but I think one has to state that during the sticky Prague summer of 1968, the era of the quiet, postwar status quo was ended. On the horizon of history the specter of a third world war has appeared, not because any great power would take chances for the sake of the Czechoslovak experiment, certainly not. But rather because the Czechoslovak crisis brought drastically to light the insolvable conflicts emerging from the division of the world in 1945.

Another result of the Soviet occupation lies in the experience which no other nation or continent has had since the time of Hitler, namely the experience of open aggression by a great power against its own ally. The actual defeat of the sovereignty of a small European state suggests the question whether it is possible in today's world to defend the sovereignty of any small state at all. The undermining of the sovereignty of African states by the economic policies of great powers is generally condemned. But the open liquidation of a sovereign European state initiated less effective action than the case of Biafra. The end of sovereign Czechoslovakia opened the way for the aggressors, and I think was accompanied by monstrous passivity on the part of the whole world including the United Nations. Not only did the United Nations not stop the aggression, they did not even make an attempt to stop it. In the International Year of Human Rights, the General Assembly accepted the most brutal violation of basic European values and humanistic traditions. For the Secretary-General it was not worth-while to visit Prague, although he many times visits places where conflicts are arising. Does this mean that the old medieval principal (cuius regio eius religio) is a new world policy of the 1960's and 1970's?

The consequences of the occupation are equally important for the Soviet bloc. The Soviet occupation proved that a Stalinist view gained a victory over the so-called revisionist or more humanistic or democratic version of socialism, over the revisionist alternatives, and it proved that the neo-Stalinists would mercilessly continue their imperialistic policy. Western people sometimes think and argue that Stalin is dead. I'm afraid the occupation has proved that Stalin is not dead, that Stalinism is alive. This neo-Stalinist policy must of course lead inevitably to a certain form of Fascism within the Soviet state. It must lead to further acts of aggression in China and elsewhere, because there is no stopping place on the road of crime once the critical point has been passed. I'm afraid the Soviet Union has passed this critical point and is becoming a criminal state. You know that criminal states end up before Nuremburg tribunals. I don't think that the invasion of Czechoslovakia is just another international crime. I'm afraid it's worse. Further, the Soviet occupation introduces methods of colonialism into Central Europe and creates a new type of colonial empire, something unbelievable twenty years ago. Brezhnev did what Stalin did not dare to do. Soviet neo-colonialism reflects a total failure of Soviet policy towards its own allies and is a testimony of incompetence to rule by means other than brute force.

The tension thus created by the Soviet Union in Europe will have far-reaching consequences in the forthcoming erosion of the Soviet system, which I hope will be the major event of the 1970's. The aggression against Czechoslovakia signals the beginning of the crisis and complete structural disintegration of the Soviet system. It is a crisis of Stalinist institutions. The Soviet intervention was not only aimed at the potential renegade but primarily against the center of possible infection. The Soviet soldiers showed also their readiness to fight the Soviet intelligentsia, which regarded the Czechoslovakian experiment as a possible alternative for its own society. A similar movement in the Soviet Union would bring about the end of the Soviet power elite, and this power elite therefore preferred the use of force, the violation of international law, the repetition of a Nazi type occupation, and the actual establishment of a Soviet protectorate. The power elite knows well that its own system is so weak that it could hardly bear the weight of the moderate liberalization which was taking place in the country of its ally. The Soviet power elite is now more dangerous than ever before, because it is frightened of its own future. And you know that people who are afraid are aggressive.

The full consequence of the Soviet aggression will not be felt immediately, although it will influence the world scene. The USSR above all offered an argument for support of the United States presence in Vietnam, which can hardly be ignored even by the most rigid opponents of the war in this country. Unfortunately, the hawks in the Kremlin support the hawks here. However, I hope that the Soviet occupation may lead to a paradoxical result, namely that it will help to end the war in Vietnam. Those in America who support the war may now realize that the real danger is not in Vietnam but in Europe. At this moment important changes can be expected on the world scene, similar to the changes which occurred in 1939—with the surprising Soviet-Nazi pact of that year. I'm afraid that the great question behind the invasion is, with whom will the USSR go? With China against the United States? Or with the United States against China?

Further, following the tragic night of August the 21st, it is impossible to maintain the naive view of the European New Left or of the American New Left, according to which, "the enemy of my enemy is my friend." Many times I have heard this slogan but I think it's completely wrong. The New Left in Europe and in America no longer has the right to ignore the fact that Castro approved the occupation of Czechoslovakia in the same way as Walter Ulbricht did. Castro is riding with Ulbricht on the same tank. Everybody for whom the slogan Mao-Castro-Ho Chi Minh represents the ultimate in political wisdom has to take into account that aggression and the spreading of Communism by armed force is identical with methods that applied to Czechoslovakia.

Now what are the consequences for Central Europe and for my country? Although the consequences of occupation are for Czechoslovakia of a limited and local nature, they do touch the very roots of the Czechoslovak state, its Communist movement

155

and both of its nations. Moreover the dialectic of history, what Hegel would call the cunning of history, creates in the heart of Europe a complicated situation that was hardly foreseen by the most enlightened politicians. The Czechoslovakia experience is of European and international importance. It's not only a local tragedy (because it's relatively unimportant how the 14 million people live in the next decade). What is important is the experience of a small state with the Soviet version of Communism. Czechoslovakia has simply proved that compromises with Stalinism do not pay. Further the Soviet occupation of Czechoslovakia means an end for state sovereignty and the establishment of a Soviet protectorate, regardless of the institutional form imposed. Czechoslovakia may follow the fate of Estonia, Latvia, Lithuania, the fate of a police state in which the fraternal Soviet police will assist in keeping order, reminding us of the atmosphere of a churchyard. It has been many times repeated that brother Brezhnev has helped brother Dubcek. We know that brother Cain also helped his brother Abel. And we know that brother Mao is prepared to help brother Brezhnev in exactly the same way.

Since midnight on August the 20th, the sovereignty of any Communist state is incompatible with membership in the Warsaw Pact. Czechoslovak policy can no longer be a policy of reform; no longer can it continue the program outlined last spring by the leadership of the Communist Party. This program for a free sovereign socialist state, for Democratic Socialism, can no longer continue in the presence of the occupation armies. Here is the greatest tragedy, and here the frustration of a great hope that we might approach a certain solution of combining European principles of democracy and socialism. The frustration of this hope is to me the most tragic aspect of the occupation.

The Soviet regime has proved that it is incompatible with human rights. Therefore any realistic policy must be based on the fact that the occupation is the end of the Czechoslovak experiment, and that no continuation is possible as long as tanks are on the territory of that country. Everything else is an open or disguised fraud. Ideals of humanism, democracy and socialism, which accompanied the creation of the Czechoslovak Republic 50 years ago (in the United States where the Czechoslovak Republic was proclaimed by a Professor of the Charles University, Thomas Masaryk)—these ideals have been exposed to a cruel test for the second time in 50 years. Munich, 1938 (and this is an unforgettable experience for every Czech and Slovak; Munich was really our national disaster) showed that there was no guarantee in the Western democracies, as far as the Czechoslovak state was concerned. By the same token the summer of 1968 proved that Czechoslovak security cannot be guaranteed by the East either. Therefore I think that any future plan for Czechoslovakia must consider the possibility of creating a broader alliance of, let us say, neutral Central European states which together would try to ensure their own security. I know that this is rather fantastic, but I believe in imagination. I think that a slogan of the students in Paris, "Imagination Pouvoir" is a good slogan for a politician who wants to see far in the future. Free Czechoslovakia is impossible with two blocs dividing Europe.

There's an unresolved issue for the nation. The question remains whether the capitulation of the army in confrontation with Russian tanks was correct. While Czech army officers were crying, young people and students without arms stood up with bare hands against the Soviet tanks. What a bizarre picture. The officers crying and a student in a tennis shoe kicking a tank. This happened in the capital of absurdity, where Kafka was born. Our nation found after 30 years another proof that capitulation without a fight does not pay. A state which does not defend itself cannot, unfortunately, exist as a state. It can exist only as a protectorate. A nation the backbone of which has been broken twice by its alleged friends, enjoys today less human rights than can be enjoyed by any new African state to whom the right to live independently is accorded as something self-evident. In defending the idea of democratic socialism, we would not have fought for any utopia, but, as I believe, for Europe's future and for European values, for

157

the basic values of man as a human being. I think there are certain situations in history where you have to accept a fight even if you cannot win. These situations in history may be rather tragic, but they exist. The problem is how you make decisions in this critical situation. I'm afraid that to break the backbone of a nation is a crime—it is worse than being defeated in a war. We had never before been so close to achieving the great ideas of some prominent men in our history and in European history as in the summer of 1968. Never before, I think, had we been so close in Europe to an authentic socialist humanism, never before had we been such an active force in history, as Hegel again would put it. But at a crucial point we gave up our consistency, we gave up the fight, we forgot the very essence of our history—the history of a European country, which, unfortunately, has to fight for its freedom if it does not want to perish.

Now what are the lessons of Prague? There are three or four points which I should like to emphasize in closing. You know there are various interpretations of what happened in Czechoslovakia, and I think a wrong one is the argument that we were only trying to introduce a certain type of Western democracy into Eastern European conditions, that the Czech experiment was a counterrevolution, or something like that. It's necessary to know what we were really trying to realize. In Prague during 1968 a splendid attempt was made to transform the political system of modern industrial society by democratic and non-violent means. This was an attempt to change economic life on a nation-wide scale, an attempt to solve human alienation, which exists everywhere in industrial society, through structural changes of the society. The foundations of this Czechoslovak experiment were crushed under tanks, but the most conspicuous lesson remained, namely that the modern effort must be an attempt to solve the crisis of the human situation in industrial societies. It must be a solution of the crisis of alienation. It must be an effort for real, as Eric Fromm calls it, de-alienation, the overcoming of alienation. The Czechoslovak experiment was an attempt to resist the consequences of the industrial production of a developed technological society through the transformation of its political superstructure.

Further, the Prague spring also proved something really unique in the history of the last 20 years: that a seemingly stable regime of a totalitarian dictatorship may be shaken by inner forces of the same totalitarian dictatorship, if a split in the leadership creates a situation where part of the power elite is forced to seek support of the population and formulate a certain humanistic program. This is very important. As soon as the capacity of the power elite is shaken, and the capacity to employ the state apparatus and its mechanisms against the democratic movement decreases, then a real possibility is established for exploiting the situation in favor of socialist democracy, for realization of human rights. I think this point is very important, because it was only through external forces that the democratization movement was stopped in Czechoslovakia. If there were an analogous movement in the Soviet Union, who would stop it? Mao?

My third point is that a revolt against dictatorship may be born out of an absurd situation where man is willing in an extreme situation to take extreme risks, because he wishes to get rid of the external anxiety, fear and humiliation. Again we see that authoritarian regimes and dictatorships create not merely all-powerful and extremely effective systems of political control, create not only efficient systems of military aggression, they also create daily the absurd situation of alienation and frustration which in a critical situation comes to the surface with surprising and seemingly incalculable force. This is, I think, a most important lesson of the Czechoslovak experiment. Dictatorships and oppressive regimes create not only oppression, but also revolting individuals and revolting masses.

Well, what will be the future of the Czechoslovak experiment? Where is the message, where is the importance, where is the historical importance of this spring, 1968? I don't know the final answer, but I think there are at least three possibilities. First of all, the message of the Czechoslovak experiment may be in the evidence that it is impossible to make Soviet Communism or the Stalinist system humanistic and European, and that this orientation called revisionism is a false doctrine which fails in front of the strategy of naked neo-Stalinist aggression. This is for me a very important theoretical and not only a practical problem, because we Czechs may have had a very noble and humanistic, perhaps an authentic and true interpretation of Marx. We had noble ideas. But we were defenseless in front of the muzzles of Soviet tanks. This is the tragedy.

Secondly, perhaps a value of the Czechoslovak spring can lie in its warning against the increasing danger of war and of further aggression. I think that the Czech crisis of today is the Soviet crisis of tomorrow.

Thirdly, it might be also true that the crisis of the Czechoslovak socialist society is, even after the defeat or through the defeat, in the process of opening new frontiers of freedom, democracy and humanism. We know from history that certain ideas were defeated many times before their final victory.

Whatever the eventualities may be, we may say that all these possibilities reflect the fate of two small nations in the heart of Europe, marching with admirable courage and with little hope towards a tragedy, appealing in vain to the conscience of the world. Because the world, if I may quote *The New York Times* of September 10th, only a fortnight after the invasion—"The World," as the headline in big letters put it, "Is Impressed by the Soviet Army in Action." Are we completely out of date, or maybe anachronistic and old-fashioned Europeans, if we still believe in the slogan of a university professor of philosophy and founder of the Czechoslovak state, Thomas Masaryk, who believed that "the Truth Prevails"? Does the truth prevail? Unpleasant philosophical and practical question. We know the answer. It's up to you to ask also, because this question is not a question for Czechs and Slovaks only, or for Europeans and Africans; this is a question for American students as well: Does the truth prevail?

European Politics: The Relations Between East and West

PROF. HASSNER: I think I'm here to provide an anticlimax, or a few relatively pedantic footnotes in guise of a framework for the central problem which should occupy us today, which is the one so well presented by Professor Svitak, namely the meaning of Czechoslovakia. I was tempted while listening to him to leave aside what I have prepared and to give my own reaction to this problem, which will I'm afraid be debated inside and outside Czechoslovakia and Europe for a long time. This problem is the various meanings of Czechoslovakia: in terms of further Soviet aggression, in terms of what should have been the Western reaction, and in terms of what should have been the reaction of the Czech government and people. I hope we'll discuss this later on. However, it may be useful for someone who is not really a Western European, who is somehow in between the two worlds, as our chairman indicated, to try—in what can only appear a much too abstract and cold way—to say how this problem fits into a wider framework, and while speaking of a lot of other things, still speak in an indirect sense mainly about Czechoslovakia.

Our topic is supposed to be "European Politics: the Relations between West and East." Personally I've been occupied with this subject under the aspect of European security—of the relationship between the political evolution of Europe and the evolution of the two great alliances, and of the role of the superpowers. I've been interested in the basic problem as to what the relationship is between domestic politics, the aspect of human and social development, and the other aspect of politics, the military balance, the interests of the great powers, and so on.

We had the impression before the Czechoslovak spring and autumn that this relationship was changing, that the relationship between political change and military security was happily such that the military problem, the security problem, was receding, and the important problem was more and more political change. Nobody really feared a war in Europe in the sense of aggression by one side against the other, and the problem twenty years after the War now seemed to involve finding a new set-up which would be more conducive to political freedom and political development. After the Czechoslovak events, one may wonder if this is still true, if after all security is as secure as we had assumed, and if change is as much around the corner as was also assumed. Perhaps we are not as well off, both in terms of security and in terms of our prospects for political change, as we had thought.

On the one hand, the vision which was beginning to gain credence held that our security problem was no longer Russia versus the West, but simply the future problem raised by Germany, and that the new European system would not be two alliances one against the other, but rather some kind of a new multilateral system, which would be agreed to by both sides and directed against no one. Today we see that the problem of balance still exists, and there may still be something to the division into two worlds, into two halves of Europe. Yet on another level it may be said that after all, much as we as persons may feel otherwise, the invasion of Czechoslovakia didn't change the situation very much. Before Czechoslovakia, if we look at the foreign policies of the Western powers (contrary to an earlier period where, for instance, France and the United States were competing for the favors of Germany through proposals like a European defense or the multilateral force) we see competition as to who will be better placed for a dialogue with Russia. What the invasion of Czechoslovakia has done is to postpone visits, to hold up the ratification of treaties by a few months. But fundamentally, it may be that the same policies and the same way of seeing the situation are as prevalent as before. There may be a kind of force in the situation, where the dialogue between the two superpowers or the search for an active role in Europe on the part of a country like France, makes them look at the Soviet Union in the same way no matter what the relationships are within the Soviet Union's own sphere.

In this respect one may say that no matter what happens from the deeper point of view of the life of people and of the structure

of societies the basic security situation in Europe is still com-
manded by the basic facts which have existed since 1945, namely
that we have a continent in the middle of which are a country
and a city which are divided by the results of World War II and
by the presence of the armies of the two great superpowers. This
fundamental situation is perhaps not really changed by what
happens on one side or the other of the dividing curtain.

My main task as I see it is thus to distinguish between the
different aspects, or the different levels, of the European situation
and of the relations between West and East in Europe.

After all, when we speak of the relations between West and
East in Europe, do we speak of the relations between Western
and Eastern Europe and of the intercourse which is created by
respective domestic changes and their mutual influence? Or do
we speak of the way in which the fundamental East-West relationship between the two great powers is reflected in Europe? The
two points of view may be very different. We may look at Europe
from the point of view of the relationship between various nations
of Europe on both sides of the Iron Curtain, and among these
the central relationship between the two Germanies, or we may
look at the relationship between the two regions of Western and
Eastern Europe, or we may look at the relationship between the
two superpowers.

It seems to me that if one looks at these three levels, the paradoxical effect (sad as it may be both for West Europeans and
East Europeans) is that for the time being the decisive thing is
not so much what happens in Western Europe or in Eastern
Europe, but rather what the relationship is between the two great
powers, both of which are at the same time European and non-
European. (You can have endless arguments as we had yesterday
whether Russia is European or not; in the same way, when one
talks about membership in a European security conference, one
always wonders whether one should follow geography and say
America is not a European power or whether one should follow
the logic of the situation and say either you have neither America

and Russia or you have both—the fact that here you have an ocean and there you have mountains doesn't really change the situation.) The important thing is precisely that the European situation is based on this ambiguous fact—that it's based on a balance in which the two main protagonists are both placed in Europe and yet have all kinds of other interests outside Europe, and all kinds of other problems.

The other central element in the situation seems to me to be the fate of Germany. As I said, the fundamental European situation is the United States and the Soviet Union facing each other in Germany—facing each other in order to balance each other, and in order to have a controlling voice over the possible future fate of Germany. It seems to me that even if one disregards ideology, Communism versus capitalism, the free world versus the Soviet world, and so on, one still has basically the situation of an unsolved German problem, you have these two powers facing each other, and in between you have a kind of more indirect, let's say more flexible, Western and Eastern European zone. But this European zone can fundamentally change the situation only to the extent to which it really affects the German problem. The reason why people are worried about de Gaulle is not so much what de Gaulle does with France, but what effect he may have on West German nationalism. The ultimate reason why, for instance, Czechoslovakia was so much more serious for the Soviet Union than, let's say, Rumania, is the effect of a contagion, or imitation, which it can produce either in East Germany or in Russia. I think that this is a fundamental situation if we look at the basic military and territorial balance, and in this respect we may say that nothing has changed since 1945.

But the problem is precisely that the world isn't simply limited to this kind of military power and geographical reality. We have two other levels, two other aspects of European politics, which are entering into collusion and collision with this basic balance. We have the level of these various states, of their diplomatic moves, of their foreign policies—of de Gaulle trying to maneuver to insert himself in the dialogue between America and Germany, between America and Russia, between Russia and Germany, to be always a kind of eternal middleman, and to make himself necessary to everything which goes on all over the place from Europe to the Middle East. We have the Rumanians trying more or less to imitate de Gaulle in Eastern Europe. We have had in the last years, since the two blocs have started to a certain extent to loosen up, a much greater apparent freedom of action at least on the level of treaties, of declarations, and various states which were not superpowers have their own policies and their own combinations. Beneath this, we have what I have mentioned already a couple of times (and which has occupied us here more than the military and diplomatic aspects), we have an undercurrent of the social and ideological transformations of populations, of generations, of beliefs, of attitudes which (and this has been one of the great lessons of the year 1968) do not respect divisions in geography or divisions in ideology. You have these undercurrents, and while you don't hear about them for years, all of a sudden they appear and transform the diplomatic and the military game itself.

One can put these three levels in a way in a kind of historic perspective, again with much simplification. One can say that for a long time it was basically the military-territorial division which was prevalent. One can say that between 1962 and 1967, after the Cuban missile crisis and the beginning of the Kennedy-Khrushchev détente, you had more and more initiative on the part of the smaller powers and of the middle powers. And you can say that 1968 has been the year when the deeper social and ideological level has all of a sudden burst into the forefront, and in a way shown that the second level, the Gaullist-type diplomacy, was in a way much more superficial, much less able to challenge the basic structure and balance, than are these relatively spontaneous and unstructured movements within states and across borders.

But what 1968 has also shown, both on the international level and in many places on the domestic level, is the ability of these structures—of the structure of the European balance, of the domination of a given country within an alliance, or the domination of a given group within a country—the ability of these power structures to reassert themselves against the assaults of the underlying currents and somehow to come back with a vengeance. While they have lost their legitimacy, their dynamism, while they have lost their claim to the enthusiasm and to the faith of their people, these structures still have the ability to stay on and to keep their domination by sheer inertia or by sheer force. This I think is really the basic problem today, the problem of the contradiction, both in West and East, between the structure based on dimensions of military and economic power, and, let us say, the social and intellectual dimension and atmosphere both within countries and within the two alliances.

In a way one may say that at least since 1962 there is something in common between West and East, namely that the presence of the two great powers and their alliance systems has never been more inevitable and at the same time never looked more obsolete. Nobody really is able to get very excited about the rhetoric either of the socialist camp or of NATO; there is no dynamic idea which can galvanize the two camps. I think Kennedy and Khrushchev each in his own way still had this excitement, but no sooner had Kennedy stopped Khrushchev's grand design in Cuba, than a month later de Gaulle stopped Kennedy's grand design by his veto of the British entry into the Common Market. Ever since, I think, the position of the great powers has been essentially defensive in Europe—it has been essentially to sit on the situation.

But on the other hand it has also been shown in 1968 that the alternatives of a Gaullist type, or in another way of a Rumanian or a Czechoslovak type, were much farther than one thought from being able to assert themselves against the existing system.

Within this situation, we have a very basic difference between the two sides. While it is true that we have the discrepancy between the superpowers and their allies on each side, in a way the situation is the opposite in the two halves of Europe. In the West one may say that there is more economic, social and cultural interdependence (or if you are anti-American, you would say more Americanization or coca-colonization). But you've also recently had a political gap. Arthur Schlesinger put it by saying, "Our pop singers sell very well in Europe, our Secretary of State sells much less well." In terms of technology, in terms of pop culture, in all kinds of ways, America supplies the dynamism and there is this interpenetration between America and Europe. But, again, there are possibilities (which one may welcome or fear) of a political separation, either because America becomes more concerned with Asia, or turns in, becoming increasingly concerned with domestic problems, or de Gaulle gets out of NATO, and so on.

In the East, it seems to me, it's exactly the opposite. In regard to the East, I would to a certain extent disagree with our chairman, and warn against the danger of seeing too much logic in the fact that Eastern Europe happens to be a unit at present. One of the central aspects of this situation, and this is especially true for Czechoslovakia and for the other Central European countries, even more than for my original country, Rumania, or Bulgaria, is the unnaturalness of this situation. The fact is that these are countries which are not Eastern countries. They were part of the Austro-Hungarian empire. Indeed, Czechoslovakia was an industrial country with the same level of development as France, where analphabetism had been wiped out by the beginning of this century, where Kafka was born, a country which was part of the history of Western Europe and of its culture, and where the people in terms of their social structure live in the same world as the West and not the East. The unnaturalness of these countries being occupied by the Soviet Union, and hence being unable to follow their natural tendency in terms of commercial orientation, in terms of cultural intercourse, in terms of intellectual and spiritual orientation, can be seen in the Czechoslovak spring. I do not suggest they will wish to adopt a Western type of economic or even political system, but rather that they do feel themselves to be in the same universe of discourse as the West. And I think it's fair to say that on the economic level, in terms of economic experiment, on the cultural level, and so on, the Soviet Union is no longer (if it ever was) a natural goal or a model for Eastern Europe. They look elsewhere, to the West or to their own creativeness—their spontaneous tendency is towards separation, towards a reorientation away from the Soviet Union. However, the Soviet Union has not the slightest intention of admitting this, has not the slightest intention of disengaging. And when an Eastern country wants to do what de Gaulle did, to get out of NATO (either actually wants to do it as the Hungarians did in 1956 or is suspected of some day wanting to do it), Soviet troops do not get out simply because they've received a letter asking them to get out, as was the case with the American troops in France. Instead, they come back or they stay on and they impose their presence.

So in one case, there is a tendency towards cultural and social and economic interpenetration along with the possibility of political and military separation. In the other case one has a cultural tendency towards divergence, towards a great deal more difference, but where the military power and will of the Soviet Union keep the bloc as it is. If this is true, then the evolution of the two parts of Europe, in spite of their present resemblances, is bound to be very different. In Western Europe, to a certain extent there is a vague logic to the whole thing. There is no illusion of having a tightly united bloc, with everything on the model of the United States; yet while political separations are possible, there are so many ties on the economic level (as we've seen with the monetary problem and so on) that these separations are not likely to develop very far. De Gaulle may have an independent foreign policy, and the United States may be tempted by Asia into semi-isolationism, but it's no more likely that there will be a complete separation than that there will be a complete identification.

But turning east again, I think it's the opposite. Precisely the most powerful state is the one which is most conservative, most resistant to change, and this is an important difference. You have additional differences in economic levels, in outlooks and so on, with the result that things are in a state of perpetual tension. As we have already seen two or three times, in Yugoslavia, Hungary, Rumania, and Czechoslovakia, as soon as the Soviet Union tries to allow a slightly more relaxed rule, to let the various countries go their own way, it all of a sudden panics because these countries quickly tend to go much too far for the Soviet taste, and the Soviet Union is afraid of the consequences for herself.

So while you have in the West, I think, a kind of muddling through, of perpetual dissatisfaction or perpetual quarrels and division, without either a completely tight bloc or a complete separation, in the East you are bound to have this periodical crisis, this pressure and desire for independence, this pressure and desire for one's own social experiments, this pressure and desire for contacts with the outside world, going to a certain point, and then being faced with the brutal reaction of the Soviet Union. Until the situation changes in the Soviet Union itself, I think one is bound to have these crises, which have dangerous implications.

Personally I do not think, as perhaps Professor Svitak implied, that the aggression against Czechoslovakia means that the Soviet Union has chosen the road of aggression everywhere, and that Czechoslovakia today is the rest of the world tomorrow. The present Soviet regime is one which mainly wants to keep what it has, which is much less adventurous than Khrushchev's. All nations today tend to go more within themselves, tend to be less interested in outside adventure or to be tired of it, and I think the Soviet Union is no exception—it is not particularly revolutionary, for example, in Latin America. But on the other hand, "turning in" for the Soviet Union means keeping its empire. As someone put it, "Socialism in One Bloc," or "Socialism in One Empire." I think the Soviet Union is in this sense trying to digest something which is indigestible, because as someone put it, in regard to Czechoslovakia Brezhnev is the greatest specialist in transplants because he has transplanted the heart of Europe onto the behind of Russia.

Thus one has a fundamentally unnatural situation, which is bound to bring tension. In other words, I think that the Soviet Empire is in a situation which is relatively analogous to the decolonization of the French or the English or in another way the American Empires. As long as it has the military power and the political will to keep its satellites, it cannot be expelled, but neither can it extinguish these satellites' aspirations for freedom. And I think there is a kind of discrepancy between this and the tendency in the West to turn inward, to turn to the problems of the cities or of the universities and so on, and to forget about foreign policy. This is fine as far it goes. But in the East the preoccupation with domestic life creates, because of the contradiction between the Soviet Union and its satellites, dangerous crises. In the West, then, we will not be prepared to channel these crises by being able to foresee them and being able to introduce this dimension both in our prediction and in our action in negotiations with Russia.

My conclusions about the present European situation involve three main points.

The first and most political point would be that for the time being the political enterprises connected with détente, with the hope of getting out of the postwar East-West system have failed. De Gaulle's policy, which was based on the prevalence of national interest over ideology, has failed. Incidentally, there are two versions of de Gaulle's Europe from the Atlantic to the Urals. You have the version according to which he thought you cannot resist a will to national independence, and hence what he represented was the reassertion both of Western European and Eastern European nations as against what he called the two hegemonies, the two imperial powers, America and Russia. Or you have the version according to which he wanted a kind of Franco-Russian understanding, wanted to substitute for America and to have a dialogue with Russia, and instead of a Europe of the two blocs to have a Europe which would be centered on the Franco-Russian relationship. I think both versions to a certain extent are true.

170

What de Gaulle wanted was, by obtaining American disengagement, to have a relative Russian disengagement, which would give more autonomy to Eastern Europe, but still would preserve a predominant Russian influence in the East and French influence in the West. In both cases de Gaulle failed, precisely because of the factor of Soviet power and especially of Soviet unwillingness to take risks in order to create a new international system.

But along with de Gaulle's failure, the other road, the road simply of having a multilateral détente, having integration, tourism, and trade, and, while keeping the framework of the two alliances, trying to erode the differences between East and West— this road has also failed in its decisive aspect. It has failed for the same reason, the prevalent power and resistance of the Soviet Union. Because the Soviet Union will always stop these evolutionary developments. Things will never go far enough, because the Soviet Union will always fear that they go too far.

So regarding the political essentials, I don't think there's much hope for change until there is a basic change in the Soviet attitude itself. This can be provoked only by a domestic liberalizing process within the Soviet Union, or by a different external constellation with China and the United States. This last might lead Russia and the United States eventually to consider that a different international system, one not based on military presence and occupation, might still give them a large enough guarantee of not having a new European war, of not having too much instability, and so on.

My second conclusion is that there exists in this ambiguous situation a basic problem as to what the West should do in terms of détente, in terms of trying to encourage Eastern Europe to adopt the same values we believe in. Since August, when I've met people from Czechoslovakia I always ask what they think the attitude of the West should be. Do they think we should have said, or should say now, to the Russians that we are all for détente, all for negotiations, for arms control, but that this presupposes that they don't behave in this way? Or is it best precisely to have as many contacts, as much friendship, as much openness as possible, so as to encourage more progressive policies, and at least to keep a window open towards the West? I have no definite answer to this problem. I think both that a détente is basically a good thing in itself, and that the thing the satellites fear most is a new cold war, which would be liable to close the system for them. At the same time, I think it is very irresponsible to promote these contacts, this openness, if one isn't prepared at the same time to back them or to protect them on the diplomatic level. We should be concerned in our relations with the Soviet Union to protect this coming together, to protect this development, by relating the Eastern European situation to every other matter which we discuss with Russia: the Middle East, the ABM, Vietnam, and so forth.

In other words, if one wants a stable and peaceful world, in which we can forget about missiles and balances of power and alliances, there must be some kind of ground rules of co-existence, not only between the two blocs and the two great powers, but also between the great powers and their smaller allies. To that extent we cannot say, "This is the Soviet sphere, we do what we want in our sphere, they do what they want in their sphere." We must work towards a world in which both by some restraint in our sphere, in situations like Vietnam or Santo Domingo, and by some (of course not military but diplomatic) intervention and concern with their sphere, we can try to promote a better situation. The great powers by necessity will have a voice in what happens in their sphere as regards security, but small countries should have their own social experiments and their own regimes. In other words, we need a situation comparable to that of Finland. Finland is a free country from the point of view of its social and political regime, but it won't enter into an alliance against the Soviet Union, and when the Soviet Union doesn't really like its foreign policy, the Finns mind their step. Thus we need to define the limits of the responsibilities of the great powers.

So I think one has both to encourage contacts and détente, but also not to have an unconditional détente, to let the Soviet Union know that their relations with us will be affected by their actions within their own sphere and their relations with their own allies.

My last point relates back to some of the earlier discussions, and also brings me back to the point from which I started, namely the relationship between two aspects of foreign policy, security and the spontaneous preoccupations of citizens in a free country. Mr. Kevin Mansell, the British student, said that to his generation the problems of European integration or not, of NATO or not, of power or not, and so forth, didn't mean very much. I am tempted to think that perhaps this is not so much a matter of generational difference, because what Mr. Mansell said was very similar to what Professor Barraclough said previously. Perhaps what these gentlemen have in common, namely their Britishness, is in this case more important than what separates them, their generation. The fact of not being interested in security and in foreign politics is a very nice luxury, which the Czechs, the Vietnamese, and many other peoples would very much like to have. It is very easy to forget about such boring and unpleasant things as the balance of power, or slowly changing the structure of a continent, and so on, if one is able to concentrate on what one is interested in—social revolution, or the university, or being left in peace by the bigger powers. When one is a Czech or a Vietnamese, foreign policy and the balance of power come to you, whether you like it or not, under the guise of tanks or of bombs. This is certainly the case for small countries today; but no country should take it for granted that it will always be free to forget about foreign policy and defense. This is only possible in an international order which permits it, and which is not obtained automatically. And in this respect I think that unless and until the structure of the international world is changed, unless and until there is a new balance which makes it more difficult for the great powers to impose their own preferences and fears on the domestic experiments and orientations of other countries, we will still have to worry about the basic European problem, which is how to reconcile the necessities of balance, the necessities of the interests of the great powers, with popular aspirations.

MR. ZAUSMER: To start off our discussion I would like to answer Dr. Svitak by saying to Czechoslovakia, the truth will prevail. It prevailed for Czechoslovakia in 1918, and 1945, and it will prevail for Czechoslovakia again. *When* is the question. Maybe I'm naive, but I don't believe it will be a generation. I'm rather pessimistic in the short run, but I'm optimistic in the long run. We can guess that the time will come when the Czechoslovak people *can* fight. To fight when you are bound to be crushed without hope of success, to me at least, does not make sense.

The New England farmers who fought the British at Lexington and Concord had a pretty good rule: "Don't fire until you see the whites of their eyes." That must have been pretty hard, but they had to do it to save ammunition. I think the Czech people have saved something much more vital than ammunition. I don't believe the Russians would have hesitated one minute to kill ten thousand or a hundred thousand people if they had had to, to destroy Czechoslovakia, its industrial facilities, its cities, and above all the most productive part of the Czech population. There would then have been nobody to stand up and fight when the time comes.

I believe that the Czechoslovak crisis of last summer, and the behavior of the Czech people, which I think was unique and remarkable, has borne fruit already for all of us. The effect on the Communist parties in Communist countries such as Rumania and Yugoslavia, and in non-Communist countries such as Italy, France, and others, has been devastating. It really marked the end of a monolithic Communist system, an end which was coming for some time. This is a pretty remarkable success which we owe the Czech people.

When the time will come that the Czech people can stand up and fight, I do not know. But I'm firmly convinced that eventually the changes which have taken place already in Yugoslavia and in Rumania, and which are taking place in the Soviet Union today in spite of the Kremlin leaders, these changes will force cooperation and a closer working together of East and West.

DR. SVITAK: I have one comment. I don't think we could have defended ourselves on that critical night—it was not possible. But I question whether we could not have prepared, whether the leadership, the Czech reformists could not have prepared the nation for active resistance or for the military defense of the republic. There was such a tendency in June and July, at the time when General Prchlík was dismissed by Dubcek. He probably wanted to prepare the country for military defense. The result of such a fight is obvious, but what was important in June and July? Well, this is an experience certainly that every girl has. Her own behavior determines the behavior of the young boy, and vice-versa. Therefore in what might be a situation of conflict, the behavior of one person depends on the behavior of the other. I think our problem and our great tragedy was that the Dubcek reformers did not prepare the country for a certain gamble, for a certain military game, trying to show that the price of the occupation would be very high. The Soviet generals, the Soviet hawks, were very undecided, even in June and July, whether to occupy the country or not. They were not, however, confronted with the situation that they might lose the battle, or that they might start a war in Europe; they were only confronted with a decision whether to occupy a defenseless country or not. You know that in the Soviet politburo very often there are tensions which might be exploited. Perhaps the Czechoslovak crisis might have stimulated a great conflict in the Soviet politburo. That was our chance. In this respect, I think that the behavior of Yugoslavia and Rumania and the other countries who showed they wouldn't give up was better than our own technique.

MR. ZAUSMER: Yugoslavia and Rumania could do this only because you suffered. It so happens that when the former Under-Secretary of State Katzenbach went to Tito to pacify him, he told him that this country would not fight for Yugoslavia. The Russians knew that too. But they still did not attack Yugoslavia or Rumania.

PROF. HASSNER: I would like to address myself primarily to the other half of our chairman's comment and agree that economic and social changes have their effect. You cannot ignore them. But the point I was trying to make is precisely that there are different forces at work: there is this force of social and economic change, but there is also the will of the leaders of the great powers, there are diplomatic combinations, and so on. I, for one, am unable to predict which of these forces will win, and how it will win. It is, I think, a too easy assumption to say that truth always prevails, that you can't in the long run go against the interests of the people. In history we remember the causes of freedom which won, but all the empires which lasted thousands of years are based on cases of freedom which lost. Even if we assume, optimistically, that in the long run world communism will die, that Soviet domination will die, all of us, too, will die in the long run. Czechoslovakia may have been a very great defeat for the Soviet Union, but with such defeats they don't need victories.

I do think there is a fundamental instability in the Soviet system. I'm sure this present regime of old aging conservative bureaucrats, who are there because they were too mediocre to be purged in 1938 when all their superiors were—I'm sure they won't sit there indefinitely. But I don't know what will succeed them, or what kind of a fight they will put up to keep themselves in power, whether there will be civil war in Russia, whether there will be a slow transition, whether there will be another Czechoslovakia —I don't know any of this. And to that extent it doesn't comfort me very much to know that the long-run trend is in a good direction.

Dr. Svitak was then asked whether the United Nations or the United States alone could have intervened in Czechoslovakia.

DR. SVITAK: First of all, I think we are the only people who are to blame for the unfortunate disaster of the outcome of the liberalization movement. I don't think that anybody in Czechoslovakia expected armed help or any military help from the Western countries, certainly not, because we knew that this would immediately produce a much more complicated situation. Nobody expected open help or military assistance before, during, or after the invasion. But the question is whether American foreign policy could have been more effective in, let us say, making the choice rather unpleasant for the Soviet Union. It's more or less only a historic possibility, a theory, but I think a strong president of the type of Kennedy would have been perhaps more interested in the central problem, that is, whether the United Nations Charter applies to Eastern Europe.

Secondly, President Johnson was in a rather critical situation. He needed Soviet help for the negotiations on Vietnam—he wanted to get rid of the Vietnamese war, and this was a difficult situation in which to provide active help.

In the third place, the American public was not prepared for any sort of diplomatic help. Since I have been here, many times I have heard from American professors and American intellectuals the statement that, "You know, we have our own problems, and we have our uncertain conscientious objections about Vietnam, we have the Dominican intervention, and problems like that, so we don't feel entitled to criticize the Russians." But I agree with the approach of many American intellectuals, that the détente should go on, if it is possible, and that contacts with Eastern intellectuals should not be broken.

So there could not have been any effective change. Regarding the Soviet politburo, if there had been a critical situation in July, with active resistance on the Czech side, if they could have expected that there would be an open war in Central Europe, maybe they would not have intervened. To open a war in Europe next to Germany, 200 kilometers from Berlin, this would be very very risky, even for the aggressive general. But I can't blame anybody for the American policy.

PROF. HASSNER: I agree with Dr. Svitak that no one should have intervened militarily or bluffed and threatened to intervene militarily. But in the critical days there was, for instance, a declaration from Dean Rusk saying that the United States doesn't want to mix itself into this situation, that what happens is of no concern. I think we could have had (as we did regarding Rumania and Yugoslavia in Johnson's speech of August 30, and in Rusk's reference at the time of the NATO Council in November) a more ambiguous stand. You don't have to make military threats, but can instead say quite publicly, quite openly, that while nobody wants to break up the Warsaw Pact, while we recognize Soviet interests, the use of force in Europe is bound to affect the future of those negotiations in which we have a mutual interest. The future of the Non-proliferation Treaty, the future of a number of things in which the Soviet Union is interested, will be affected. And one can say that in broader terms the United States may be led to look with a more open eye towards certain possibilities about which the Russians are very sensitive, like Sino-Soviet relations, where they always claim or affect to claim that they are very afraid of an American-Chinese understanding. You don't threaten war on anybody, but simply say this whole train of negotiations of mutual interest might be endangered. This might (nobody will know) have had an effect. At any rate it should have been tried for Czechoslovakia, as it was for Rumania and Yugoslavia. Nobody can prove that it would have changed something for Czechoslovakia, or that this attitude is the determining factor regarding Rumania and Yugoslavia. But I think this policy is preferable to the one followed in the first case.

Dr. Svitak was then asked to compare the alliance among Czechoslovak students and workers with the desires for such an alliance in Western Europe.

DR. SVITAK: I have written an article about this which will appear in *New Politics* in the next issue. I want to say that there is a great difference between the student movement in Eastern Europe and in the Western European countries. I think the most important difference is that the Western students' movement, the radical movement, is rather isolated. The students in Prague constantly expressed certain ideas which represented the national feeling, the feeling and desperation of the whole nation. And now the self-immolation of Jan Palach exactly expresses the tragic and absurd situation of the whole nation. Therefore he's a national hero.

Another important difference is that the Czechs were fighting not for national interests, not for specific interests, rather we were trying to stress a human aspect and a humanist program, human rights. The Declaration of Human Rights was the most widely-read and most important political document for us. American students mostly do not realize what it means to live in a totalitarian dictatorship. They protest against oppressive aspects of what they might call a capitalist or an industrial society, but, you know, the difference between a society in which you *have* elementary human rights and one in which you *haven't* is very deep. Radical students who do not understand this difference are completely under-estimating the Fascist or the totalitarian danger. When Rudi Dutschke came to Prague last Easter, the reaction of the Czech students at the Charles University, the reaction of radical students was to laugh at him. They couldn't take him seriously. He was speaking about what the system should be like, and what democracy meant, and yet he was at the same time applying totalitarian concepts. The students sitting there knew exactly what it means to live for twenty years under a totalitarian dictatorship, and they told him, well, you are so conservative, you are so dogmatic, that you are worse than our party secretary. We wouldn't like you to be our party secretary, because the party secretary is more liberal than you are. That's the difference, I think.

The discussion then shifted to the topic of German unification, Prof. Hassner being asked for his opinion on the long-run prospects, and how West Germans and Europeans in general reacted to the problem.

179

PROF. HASSNER: This is the 64 dollar question for the future of Europe, once the more barbaric aspect which we are talking about in connection with Czechoslovakia is hopefully removed. Even a Russia in which domestic changes have occurred could never lose its preoccupation with the future of Germany.

Today the possibilities for German unification are extremely feeble. If I had to bet, I would say that in the foreseeable future Germany will not be unified, at least in the sense of there being a German state made up of the two present Germanys. But I don't like to be dogmatic, because very often we have tended to think, for example, that in Communist regimes there was a stabilization and an acceptance developing in the population, only to be surprised as new possibilities appear. And on the Western side we have assumed that people are happily concentrating on domestic politics, on prosperity and so on, only to be surprised by new waves either of nationalism or of interest in foreign politics. So I suppose it is not impossible that if the road block to unification were suddenly removed people might suddenly think in different terms. We've often seen how people can act and feel and believe differently in a matter of months, once a situation starts developing its own dynamics. I would simply say that today the prospect is very bleak, and neither Europeans nor Germans really expect unification. But nobody is sufficiently certain that if we had the two German states without the presence of the Americans and the Russians—or some other framework, for instance European integration, which might replace them—that these two German states would remain there peacefully without wanting either to reunite or to fight each other. Would they remain just separate enough not to want to merge and just friendly enough not to be hostile to each other? It's possible. But for the time being everyone else prefers to keep the present situation, and not to take chances with this future situation.

Dr. Svitak was then questioned as to whether he felt a move-

ment similar to the Czech reform movement could develop in the Soviet Union.

DR. SVITAK: Five years ago, a person with a great imagination, let us say with the imagination of Salvador Dali, couldn't expect that something like what has happened in Czechoslovakia would happen. If we have the surrealist imagination of this great painter, I think we can imagine that internal crises, especially economic crises (because this was the Gordian knot of the Czechoslovak crisis) could occur. An economic crisis produces certain tendencies, elementary trends, which can't simply be solved by political means. They can't be solved by the police and by the army. We see certain aspects of events in the Soviet Union which are very analogous to the situation in 1965 or 1966 in Czechoslovakia. Of course, there are only isolated individuals, who seem to be nearly crazy because they protest against some sort of violence. There was, for instance, the demonstration on Red Square on the 21st. Isolated phenomena, you may say, but nevertheless they exist and this perhaps shows a tendency. The intellectual ferment in Russia is so important for this reason. Everybody who understands the structure of the regime knows that the Soviet power elite is afraid of this intellectual ferment, knows that it is just, and knows that this ferment is very very important. These people have no force, they do not represent anything, except to say that there is something wrong in the structure of the system. The Sakharov Manifesto—maybe some of you have read it—it's extremely important, and it shows the atmosphere of the whole society.

Now I believe that such a trend exists as a latent possibility in the Soviet regime. Therefore I am not pessimistic about the future evolution of the Soviet Union, about the Soviet intelligentsia. I believe in the Russian intellectuals, I think they might help us. They are really European. The great Vadim Delonfe, the man who put on a demonstration in the Red Square, said to the Russian attorney, "Well, for three minutes on the Red Square I was free, and now I will pay for it for three years." *He's* the European in Russia!

Prof. Hassner was asked to discuss the role of Western European Communist opinion in the Czechoslovak incident.

PROF. HASSNER: I might tie this with the question which was just discussed, in terms of the psychology of the Soviet leaders. While of course they would prefer not to have opposition in the Western Communist parties, basically there are plenty of reports that they treated this with contempt. They perhaps felt there is no hope of Communism coming to power in Western Europe anyway, and perhaps that these are not real Communists—they have become Social Democrats.

In other terms, I think they have made the basic choice that it is much more important to keep what one has. To the extent that the leaders of the Soviet Union become less ideological, this is no comfort at all to Eastern Europe. Rather the contrary, because the more they discount the progress of revolution in the rest of the world the more they want to keep what they have. In general (and this is why again I am not optimistic) this is an outlook which to a certain extent the great masses of the population in the Soviet Union share with their leaders. The great difference between the Soviet Union and Eastern Europe is the very great isolation of the intellectuals in the Soviet Union. One sees this very often in their own descriptions. But as Professor Svitak said, the great thing about students and intellectuals and the young people in Czechoslovakia was that they had the support of the unions, of the mass of the population. In some places like Poland there are tensions right now. But in Russia, I think, the intellectuals are very often regarded as unpatriotic cranks, and there is a certain community of feeling between the bureaucratic power elite and the average man in the street. The average Russian thinks, "We are a great power. These Czechs are ungrateful people, whom we liberated and who now are treating us badly."

This is the question: to what extent will the intellectual ferment really produce desired changes? Or will it produce a counter-reaction of the party elite and the military, with the people failing to take their place at the side of the intellectuals?

Dr. Svitak was asked to discuss the "Brezhnev Doctrine."

DR. SVITAK: The Brezhnev Doctrine is something absolutely new. This is really an open doctrine of Soviet—well, I don't know what to call it—neo-Stalinism or neo-colonialism, neo-fascism, or what. Even Stalin or Lenin never said this is a part of the official policy of the Soviet Union. I'm very much afraid of this trend, because the inner conflict in the Soviet Union produced the old solution, which is to start a war, to start occupying other countries. Once you start this aggressive trend, you can't stop. Hitler could not stop in 1939. In the 1930's, very clever statesmen, the leading statesmen in England, thought Hitler had a certain exaggerated nationalism, or that he went too far. But these stories about concentration camps, that he was murdering the Jews, they thought that was just nonsense, just exaggerated propaganda. How many people believed in 1944 that there were really concentration camps where people are exterminated? How many people believed in 1945, in my country and in America also, that there were concentration camps in the Soviet Union? I remember a book by Dallin—it was the first book about Soviet forced labor, and its estimate was that between 3 and 15 million people in the country were in the Soviet concentration camps. I couldn't believe it! I thought, well, it's anti-communist propaganda, certainly exaggerated. But Koestler and some other people knew the reality. Sometimes reality is so unacceptable, it's so terrifying, that you want to resist it. Unfortunately, people who know Russia, who know the Soviet system, who know the logic of the system, are rather pessimistic and will say something worse than I do. You know, Djilas came to the United States immediately after the invasion, and he said it's up to you to decide whether it's not better to fight at the Adria than on the Channel, it's up to you to decide. Djilas had personal discussions with Stalin; he knows. And George Kennan, who knows something about Russia, was very skeptical as well. So I'm afraid of the trend.

Prof. Hassner was asked whether West German policy initiatives had had any influence on the events in Czechoslovakia, and whether West German non-recognition of the Oder-Neisse line was in any way related.

PROF. HASSNER: I think practically every non-German person in the world, and an increasing number of Germans as well, are for the recognition of the Oder-Neisse line. But I don't think that there is any direct relationship between this point and the Czechoslovak invasion. The interesting point is rather the opposite, that when the Germans quite rightly, upon the prompting of everyone else, started being more for détente, and began revising their policies, this is what provoked a very hostile Soviet reaction, because precisely what the Soviets fear above all else is a reconciliation between Germany and Eastern Europe. One could see this also in Poland when on the occasion of the millennium celebrations, the bishops emphasized the theme of forgiveness. When the population followed them, the Communist party came out very strongly against it. It creates problems for the Russians when there is a progressive West German policy instead of a reactionary one.

Dr. Svitak was then asked to elaborate on what he meant by the Czech humanization of the Marxist system.

DR. SVITAK: Here in America you often identify Communism with Marxism and the Soviet system with Marxism. I don't think it is a Marxist system at all. If you read Marx, you know what Marx really wanted. For Marx it was absolutely unimaginable to combine a system which called itself socialistic with the nonexistence of human rights. For him elementary human rights—this was something obvious, because he was a man of the 19th century, he hadn't experienced totalitarian dictatorship. If you know Marx, you find in the Soviet Union the most anti-Marxist policy you can imagine. So I wouldn't combine these two ideas.

What was important in Czechoslovakia was the interpretation that we were and are trying to give to Marxism, to show the elementary core of Marx, the authentic Marx, which is really humanism. If you follow the evolution of the young Marx, you will see that his doctrine was practically an attempt to apply the European ideas of humanism, and, let us say, the idea of a utopian future to the present society. Trying to interpret Marxism as a humanist doctrine is very important in Eastern Europe, where you have no other chance to attack the dogmatist interpretation, the unhuman Stalinist ideology which has nothing to do with Marxism. The Soviet ideology is rather consistent, and you have no other intellectual possibility than to try to approach the problem through Marx, through Marxist humanism. That's exactly what the Yugoslavs are doing, and the Poles in the 1950's, and that's what we are doing.

I think we are rather close to the reality. Marx was a great genius of the 19th century, but unfortunately if we try to act by his ideas in the 20th century, and not respect the specific aspects of modern history, we simply come to wrong conclusions. Marx was certainly one of the greatest in the 19th century, but the truth is more important. There is a greater force than Marx, and this is truth. Truth, reason, is the real revolutionary force in the cosmos, it is the most important force. I believe in reason. I believe in truth, and I hope that the truth will prevail.

SPEAKERS

ARNULF BARING is currently a research fellow in the German Research Program and Research Associate of the Center for International Affairs, Harvard University. He has been offered the John F. Kennedy Chair of Political Science at the Free University, West Berlin, and will also direct a research institute in comparative politics there. Dr. Baring received his training in law and politics at the Free University, the Universities of Hamburg and Freiburg, and Columbia University. He also studied at the Institute for Administrative Science in Speyer, Germany, and at the Fondation Nationale des Sciences Politiques in Paris. He has taught at the Free University and the Otto Suhr Institute, and has been political editor of the West German Broadcasting System. His books include *Charles de Gaulle: His Greatness and Limits; The 17th of June, 1953,* and *Foreign Policy in a Chancellor-Democracy: Konrad Adenauer and the European Defense Community.* He has published numerous articles and reviews in such German publications as *Die Zeit, Der Monat, Neue Politische Literatur,* and *Juristenzeitung.*

GEOFFREY BARRACLOUGH, Professor of History at Brandeis University, has also taught at Oxford, Cambridge, the University of Liverpool, the University of London, and the University of California. He has served in the British Foreign Office and with the Royal Air Force. Professor Barraclough is a past President of the

Historical Association of the United Kingdom. His many publications include *The Origins of Modern Germany; Survey of International Affairs; History in a Changing World,* and *European Unity in Thought and Action.*

GUIDO CALOGERO, a Professor of Philosophy at the University of Rome, has also taught at the Universities of Florence and Pisa. Outside of Italy, Professor Calogero has taught at McGill University and at the University of California, Berkeley, served as Director of the Institute of Italian Culture, London, from 1950 to 1955, and has been associated with the International Institute of Philosophy in Paris. A politician as well as a scholar, Professor Calogero was a member of the committee charged with writing the Constitution of the Italian Republic after World War II. He has written extensively on political affairs for various newspapers, including *Il Mondo,* and is currently involved in the movement for university reform in Italy. His many books include *The School of Man; Esthetics, Semantics and History; Justice and Liberty; Defense of Liberal Socialism,* and *Lessons of Philosophy.*

ALEXANDER GERSCHENKRON, Professor of Economics, Harvard University, is currently a fellow at the Institute for Advanced Study, Princeton. Professor Gerschenkron has served as Research Associate for the Austrian Institute for Business Cycle Research, has been the Director of Economic Projects of the Russian Research Center, Harvard, and has served on the staff of the Board of Governors of the Federal Reserve System. He has been Ford Research Professor at the University of California, Berkeley, and a Guggenheim Fellow. His publications include *Continuity in History and other Essays; Economic Backwardness in Historical Perspective; Bread and Democracy in Germany; Economic Relations with the U.S.S.R.,* and many articles in scholarly journals.

PIERRE HASSNER is Research Associate at the Centre D'Etude des Relations Internationales, Fondation Nationale des Sciences Politiques, Paris, and is Visiting Professor of International Politics at the Johns Hopkins University Center, Bologna, Italy. He has written extensively on problems of German and European reunification, and security and stability in world politics, publishing in such journals as *Survey* and the *Adelphi Papers* of the Institute for Strategic Studies. Professor Hassner is co-author of *Diplomacy in the West*.

JAN KAVAN has played a leading role in Czechoslovak student affairs, currently being the Head of the Section for Foreign Relations of the Union of University Students of Bohemia and Moravia (S.V.S.). He has represented S.V.S. at many conferences in other European nations and the United States, has appeared on several B.B.C. broadcasts, and has published in *Ramparts, Student,* and several other journals.

CHARLES P. KINDLEBERGER is currently Professor of Economics at the Massachusetts Institute of Technology. In the past he has been associated with the Bank for International Settlements, the Federal Reserve Bank of New York, the Board of Governors of the Federal Reserve System, and the Department of State. He has written *Europe's Postwar Growth; Europe and the Dollar; Foreign Trade and the National Economy; Economic Growth of France and Britain; Economic Development; International Economics,* and several other works.

EKKEHART KRIPPENDORFF was associated with various student groups, including the S.D.S., while a student in Germany. After graduating, he was a teaching assistant at the Free University, Berlin, and a member of the left-wing Republican Club, an extra-parliamentary opposition group. He has been a Fulbright postgraduate Fellow in the United States, teaching at Yale, and is currently a Visiting Professor of Political Science at Queens College, the City University of New York. Dr. Krippendorff has written *The Liberal Democratic Party in East Germany, 1945–8,* edited *American Political Science,* and published in various scholarly and popular journals in West Germany.

UGO LA MALFA is currently a member of the Italian Chamber of Deputies, and is General Secretary of the Republican Party. He has held various positions in the Italian government, including those of Minister of Transport, Minister of Reconstruction, Minister Without Portfolio, Minister of Foreign Trade, and most recently Budget Minister. Signor La Malfa has also been active in the movement for European unification, served as Vice-Governor of the International Monetary Fund, was a member of the Strasbourg Assembly, and in 1948 headed the Italian delegation sent to Moscow to work out commercial agreements with the U.S.S.R. Before the war, he was associated with the Bank of Sicily and the Commercial Bank of Italy. Politically, Signor La Malfa was a leader of the Action Party, an outgrowth of the Italian Resistance, and now plays an important role in the Republican Party, which is one of the parties in Italy's Center-Left coalition. A contributor to the *Encyclopedia Treccani,* Signor La Malfa's books include *Italian Economic Policy, 1946–52; Against de Gaulle's Europe; Towards A Planned Politics,* and most recently *The Ideology and Policy of a Left Wing Force.*

WALTER LAQUEUR currently divides his time between Great Britain, where he is director of the Institute of Contemporary History, The Wiener Library, London, and the United States, where he is Professor of the History of Ideas and Politics, Brandeis University. He has also taught at Harvard, the University of Chicago, and the Johns Hopkins University. Professor Laqueur is the founder and past editor of *Survey,* is currently co-editor of *The Journal of Contemporary History,* and has published in *Commentary, The New York Times, Twentieth Century* and many other journals. His books include *The Fate of the Revolution: Interpretations of Soviet History; Young Germany; Poly-Centrism, the New Factor in International Communism; Left Wing Intellectuals Between the Wars; Future of Communist Society; Literature and Politics in the Twentieth Century; Road to Jerusalem* and many other works on the Middle East.

KEVIN MANSELL is a former Vice Chairman of the Student Representative Council, Cambridge University, serving also as a delegate to the British National Union of Students. He is currently a graduate student in economics at Yale University.

IVAN SVITAK holds Doctorates in Law, Philosophy, and Political Science. He has taught at the Charles University, Prague, and other Czechoslovak universities, is a member of the Institute of Philosophy, Czechoslovak Academy of Science, Prague, and is currently a Senior Fellow at the Research Institute on Communist Affairs, Columbia University. Professor Svitak has published articles in *Survey, Student, East Europe, Orbis* and other journals, and is the author of *History of Philosophy; Voltaire as a Humanist; Human Sense of Culture,* and other works. His forthcoming books include *The Human Meaning of Marxism* and *The Czechoslovak Experiment.*

WILLARD THORP has held many important positions in the United States government including those of Chairman of the Advisory Council of N.R.A., advisor to the Secretary of Commerce, Director of the Bureau of Foreign and Domestic Commerce, and Deputy Assistant Secretary of State for Economic Affairs. He was Assistant Secretary of State in the Truman administration. Dr. Thorp has also been a United States delegate to the United Nations General Assembly and to UNESCO, and has been Chairman of the American delegation to G.A.T.T. A graduate of Amherst College, Dr. Thorp was Professor of Economics and also served as Acting President and Trustee of that institution. He has also been associated with the research staff of Dun and Bradstreet, Inc., and recently has been Director of the National Bureau of Economic Research. Dr. Thorp has also recently been Chairman of the Development Assistance Committee of the Organization for Economic Cooperation and Development (O.E.C.D.), Paris. His publications include *Trade, Aid, or What?; Economic Problems in a Changing World,* and *Development Assistance Efforts and Policies.*

LARS F. TOBISSON is a past President of the Swedish National Union of Students. He attended the University of Göteborg, graduating with a candidate's degree in philosophy, and is currently associated with the Central Organization of Swedish Professional Workers. He has published an article dealing with the Student Union, "Ergo International," in the book, *The Intellectual Face of Sweden.*

ERIC VAN LOON, currently a first year student at the Harvard Law School, became involved in student affairs while an undergraduate at the University of North Carolina. In his senior year he served on the National Supervisory Board of the National Student Association. Last year, while studying at the London School of Economics and Politics, he was the N.S.A.'s Overseas Representative. He has participated in a Ford Foundation Seminar at Vanderbilt University, and has written for *Student* and *American Education.*

OTTO ZAUSMER joined the *Boston Globe* in 1939, serving successively as Foreign Correspondent, Editorial Writer, and Editor of the Editorial Page, and is now Associate Editor. During World War II he was Deputy Chief of Intelligence for the Office of War Information, London. A Viennese by birth, he received a Doctorate in Philology, in which field he has published three books and a number of articles.